P9-CSB-191

UNFORGETTABLE CHARACTERS

Reader's Digest Paperbacks

Informative.....Entertaining.....Essential.....

Berkley, one of America's leading paperback publishers, is proud to present this special series of the best-loved articles, stories and features from America's most trusted magazine. Each is a one-volume library on a popular and important subject. And each is selected, edited and endorsed by the Editors of Reader's Digest themselves! Watch for these others . . .

DRAMA IN REAL LIFE®
THE LIVING WORLD OF NATURE
WORD POWER

Berkley/Reader's Digest books

THE ART OF LIVING
DRAMA IN REAL LIFE®
"I AM JOE'S BODY"
THE LIVING WORLD OF NATURE
SECRETS OF THE PAST
TESTS AND TEASERS
UNFORGETTABLE CHARACTERS
WORD POWER

THE EDITORS OF *READER'S DIGEST*

Unforgettable Characters

A BERKLEY/READER'S DIGEST BOOK
published by
BERKLEY BOOKS, NEW YORK

UNFORGETTABLE CHARACTERS
A Berkley/Reader's Digest Book, published by arrangement with Reader's
Digest Press

PRINTING HISTORY
Berkley/Reader's Digest edition/November 1980

All rights reserved.
Copyright © 1980 by The Reader's Digest Association, Inc. Copyright
© 1935, 1937, 1940, 1943, 1945, 1946, 1947, 1949, 1950, 1951, 1952,
1953, 1954, 1956, 1957, 1958, 1959, 1960, 1961, 1962, 1963, 1964,
1967, 1968, 1969, 1970, 1971, 1973, 1974, 1975, 1976, 1977, 1978,
1979 by the Reader's Digest Association, Inc.
Cover design by Sam Salant.
This book may not be reproduced in whole or in part, by mimeograph or
any other means, without permission.
For information address: Berkley Publishing Corporation, 200 Madison
Avenue, New York, New York 10016.

ISBN: 0-425-04722-9

A BERKLEY BOOK ® TM 757,375
PRINTED IN THE UNITED STATES OF AMERICA

Acknowledgments

Grateful acknowledgment is made to the following organizations and individuals for permission to reprint material from the indicated sources:

The Oregonian (October 2, 1975; March 4, April 8, May 6, June 3 and July 8, 1976) for "A Gift for Mama" by Helene Melyan, copyright © by Oregonian Publishing Co.; The Lantz Office Incorporated for "Courage, and Farewell!" condensed from PROMISE AT DAWN by Romain Gary, copyright © 1961 by Romain Gary.; Ms. Jeanmarie Coogan for "So You're Kate's Girl" which originally appeared in the Ladies' Home Journal October 1962.; Random House, Inc. for "Life Is a Banquet" from LIFE IS A BANQUET by Rosalind Russell and Chris Chase, copyright © 1977 by Frederick Brisson, as an individual and Frederick Brisson, Executor of The Estate of Rosalind Russell. Reprinted by permission of Random House, Inc.; *Esquire* for "Elvis the Man" condensed from the article "Elvis" by Jon Bradshaw copyright © 1977 by Esquire Magazine Inc.; *Milwaukee Journal* (December 26, 1976) for "... And the Elvis Mystique" by Alice Anne Conner, copyright © 1976 by The Milwaukee Journal; William Morrow & Company for "Mike Malloy vs. the Murder Trust" from THE

PEOPLE'S ALMANAC #2 by David Wallechinsky and Irving Wallace. Copyright © 1978 by David Wallechinsky and Irving Wallace. By permission of William Morrow & Company; Farrar, Straus and Giroux, Inc. for "Secrets of a Soviet Assassin" from the book THE MIND OF AN ASSASSIN by Isaac Don Levine, copyright © 1959 by Isaac Don Levine; Charles Scribner's Sons and The Hamlyn Publishing Group Ltd. for "A Troublesome Boy" from A ROVING COMMISSION (MY EARLY LIFE) by Winston S. Churchill. Copyright © 1930 Charles Scribner's Sons; renewal copyright © 1958 Winston Churchill. Originally published by Odhams Press Ltd.; *American Heritage Magazine* (December 1955) for "The Washed Window" by Dorothy Canfield Fisher, copyright © 1955 by American Heritage Pub. Co., Inc.; *Kiwanis Magazine* (September 1943) for "The Lives & Loves of the Siamese Twins" by J. P. McEvoy, copyright © 1943 Kiwanis International; Hawthorn Books, Inc. for "The Extraordinary Story of Helen Keller" from JOURNEY INTO LIGHT by Ishbel Ross, copyright © 1950 by Appleton-Century-Crofts, Inc. Reprinted by permission of Hawthorn Books, Inc.; Simon & Schuster for "Diamond Jim" from DIAMOND JIM: THE LIFE AND TIMES OF JAMES BUCHANAN BRADY by Parker Morell, copyright © 1934 by Parker Morell and published by Simon & Schuster; Mr. Cleveland Amory for "Last of the Old-Time Shooting Sheriffs." *Louisville Magazine* (January 1975) for "Saga of the 'Chicken' Colonel" by James Stewart-Gordon, copyright © 1974 by The Louisville Area Chamber of Commerce Inc.; Harper & Row, Publishers, Inc. for "Behind The Legend of Babe Ruth" from HOW THE WEATHER WAS by Roger Kahn, copyright © 1973 by Roger Kahn. Reprinted by permission of Harper & Row, Publishers, Inc.; *Saturday Evening Post* (March 1977) for "Most Daring Woman on Earth" by Phil Bowie, copyright © 1977 by The Saturday Evening Post Co.; *The New York Times* (February 8, 1970) for "A Champion Tenor Defends His Title" by William Honan, copyright © 1970 by The New York Times Company. Reprinted by permission of The New York Times Company; The Nicholas Literary Agency and New York Sunday News Magazine (November 30, 1975) for "My Father's Hands" by Calvin R. Worthington, copyright © 1975 by New York News, Inc.; Alfred A. Knopf, Inc. for "God and My Father" by Clarence Day. Copyright © 1931 by Clarence Day and renewed 1959 by Katherine B. Day. Reprinted from THE BEST OF CLARENCE DAY, by permission of Alfred A. Knopf, Inc.; Macmillan Publishing Co., Inc. for "My Quicksilver Uncle" by Robert P. Tristram Coffin. Condensed with permission of Macmillan Publishing Co., Inc. from BOOK OF UNCLES by Robert P. Tristram Coffin. Copyright © 1942 by Macmillan Publishing Co., Inc., renewed 1970 by Margaret Coffin Halvosa.

Contents

Womanly
Instincts

A Gift for Mama
by *Helene Melyan*

There is a country—I read about it once—where the local custom is that if you go to a house and praise some small possession, the owners feel obliged to offer it to you as a gift. I don't remember the name of the country; the only other place I know of with such a custom is my mother's apartment.

Knowing Mama, I have always been careful with my compliments, but that doesn't stop her. Mama senses admiration far more subtle than the spoken compliment. If she catches me staring at anything small enough to put in a grocery sack, she hands it to me as I leave. It would do no good to protest, "I was merely staring at that photograph of Mt. Hood because I have one exactly like it in my living room." Mama would only nod and say, "Of course. You were thinking how nice it would be to have a set. If a mother doesn't understand, who does?"

Sometimes, while visiting Mama and trying not to say or

do anything complimentary, I reflect on what might have been. I have visions of her in the White House, bidding her dinner guests farewell: "Here you are, Mr. Prime Minister, that nice picture of George Washington you were admiring so much, from the Blue Room. No, take it, you like it—what do I need it for?"

Being with Mama is different, like watching an Alfred Hitchcock movie: I never know what's going to happen next. For instance, I have lasting memories of childhood walks with her. Mama noticed everything we passed. We had to stop to admire a nice house, a nice tree, a nice flower. Mama regarded the people we saw (those who didn't look like her relatives) as portraits in a museum—no matter if people stared back. "She was pretty once, but has seen tragedy," Mama would whisper, or, "Such a handsome man, but conceited to the core." Her sharpest epithet was "Minky," reserved for the type of woman Mama thought would wear a mink to the supermarket.

As far back as I can remember, Mama was telling people they were in the wrong line of work, and suggesting alternative careers. If the landlord fixed the sink, she told him he should have been a plumber. If he couldn't fix it, Mama would wait until the plumber came and then tell him he should have been a landlord. And if either one of them told her a joke while he was putting his tools away, Mama would have to know why he hadn't gone into show business.

My turn was to come, when I grew up and became a housewife. "You missed your calling," Mama sighs, examining the doodles on my phone book. "You should have been an artist." Later, I tell her how I returned rancid fish to the supermarket and demanded a refund, and she amends this to "lawyer." I know it's horsefeathers, but I like it.

"You missed *your* calling," I tell Mama. "You should have been a vocational counselor."

"I know," she sighs. "But that's life. Maybe now that it's spring..."

According to Mama, there is no problem that will not be a little bit solved by the coming of spring. I grew up believing that there was only one correct way to end a discussion of things unpleasant or troublesome: nod at the calendar, pat somebody on the back if possible, and sigh, "Maybe in the spring..."

I could understand how certain problems—sinus conditions, chapped lips, sticking windows—would be expected to respond to the change of seasons. But I never tried to unravel the spring magic that Mama vowed would help me understand fractions or long division.

I was not the only target of Mama's philosophy. At one time or another, Mama had several dozen people in the neighborhood waiting for spring to relieve them of indigestion, mice, domestic difficulties, and trouble with the horizontal hold on their television sets.

Sometimes, sitting in school during history (which Mama promised me I'd find less boring in the spring), I would daydream my mother into other places and other times. Once I saw her patting Napoleon on the back, after he got the news from the Russian front. ("Wait. Maybe in spring . . .") She was beside George Washington at Valley Forge, brushing snow off his epaulets. ("In spring, maybe, you'll win the Revolution. I wouldn't worry about it.") She was looking over Edison's shoulder, comforting him in his early failures. ("Don't worry, maybe in the spring you'll try something new. Everything will be all right.")

I have been worrying for weeks now about what to give my mother for Mother's Day. For most people this is a modest problem, solved by the purchase of a bathrobe or a box of candy. For me, however, Mother's Day represents an annual challenge to do the impossible—find a gift that will make neither Mama nor me feel terrible.

Expensive gifts—which Mama defines as costing over $1.98—are out, because they make Mama feel terrible. ("This is awful," she says, examining an apron. "I feel just terrible. You shouldn't have spent the money on me.") Inexpensive presents—under $1.98—please Mama, but they make *me* feel terrible.

There is always the danger a gift given to Mama will bounce swiftly back to the giver. If I buy her something wearable, she perceives in an instant that it could be let in here, let out there, and it would fit me perfectly. If I give her a plant, she cuts off the top for me to take home and root in a glass of water. If I give her something edible, she wants me to stay for lunch and eat it.

Papa, a sensible man, long ago stopped trying to shop for

Mama. Instead, on Mother's Day, her birthday and other appropriate occasions, he composes for her a short epic poem in which he tells of their meeting, courtship and subsequent marriage. After nearly 30 years of poems, Papa sometimes worries that the edge of his poetic inspiration has dulled, but Mama doesn't complain. She comes into the room while he is struggling over a gift poem and says, "It doesn't have to rhyme, as long as it's from the heart."

This year, finally, I think I too have found a painless gift for Mama. I am going to give her a magazine article, unrhymed but from the heart, in which I wish her "Happy Mother's Day," and tell her there's nothing Papa or I could ever buy, find or make her that would be half good enough, anyway.

"How I Haff Suffered!"
by Carole Gaffron

For years our family had no name. We were simply "the people who have Meta." She was practically a legend in our neighborhood; few understood how my mother could put up with her. Although I am now a grown woman with a family of my own, Meta still looms an awesome figure in my memory. She was not, outwardly at least, a lovable woman; as children, my brother and I were terrified of her. Yet she taught us more, in her own inimitable way, about trust and love and loyalty than any book, any school, any single person I know.

Meta had been our housekeeper long before I was born. It seemed as though she had always been there, like the picture of my grandmother which had hung for decades in the hall. Skinny as a pole, with sharp blue eyes, an austere face, and wispy gray hair drawn tight into a bun, she had come over from Germany in the 1920s. In spite of the 40-odd years she spent in this country, she could barely speak English. I always remember her as being dried up and old, like a piece of yellow rice paper. Yet she was constantly reminding us of how beautiful she had been as a girl. "Plump I vass, mitt fat red cheeks, and mine hair vass so beautiful—shining and long, haff-vay down mine back." She insisted that our family made her "t'in and ugly," especially my older brother, Edward, and me. *We* had melted away the very flesh from her bones. "Ach!" she would cry, rolling her eyes and lifting her hands, "How I haff suffered here!"

Yet she stayed on for 34 complaining years.

My mother was Spanish, and her English was almost as poor as Meta's. It is one of life's mysteries how they managed to converse. There was a sort of mystic radar between them, unfathomable to the rest of us, which enabled them to understand each other, despite the disjointed vocabulary and garbled syntax. In self-defense, my brother and I would often joke about Meta's English, thereby touching off an explosion of unintelligible German. Yet once when I laughed at something my mother had said, Meta gave me a tongue-lashing I never forgot.

"She iss your Mama," she cried heatedly. "You no make fun of de vay she talk. You haff respect for her—you hear me? Good English no make a good Mama!"

Better Than the FBI. Meta fought with everybody: my brother, me, even at times my parents. "Old Maid Grump," the neighborhood children called her. She was difficult to please. At Christmas and on her birthdays, we used to give her scarves, gloves, nightgowns—once, I remember, a beautiful Spanish shawl—but she would merely unwrap each gift, grunt, and abruptly put it away. I never recall her wearing any of them, even once. After a while we discovered that money was the only present she really wanted. Cash, it seemed, was the one thing Meta truly respected.

As a matter of fact, Meta was so thrifty that my mother had to keep constant watch. Left to herself, she would buy only the cheaper cuts of meat, and there was never enough food in the refrigerator.

There was only one member of our family that Meta worshiped: our Boston terrier, Gigi. I remember one afternoon on

Meta's day off (my mother was away), my father was rummaging around in the kitchen looking for something to eat. In the refrigerator he came upon a small cube steak carefully wrapped. But before he had a chance to find a pan, he heard that formidable clump! clump! on the stairs. In less than a second Meta had whisked the steak right out of his hand.

"No, dat's for Gigi!" she cried indignantly. "Here, you can haff de chop meat!"

My father tried to protest that hamburger was perfectly fine for dogs. She looked at him in horror. "Vat—you vant to *poison* her?"

My father ate the hamburger.

Despite numerous threats, Meta left us only once. At the end of World War II she accepted a job with another family who had offered her a substantial raise in salary. She had been there only a week when she slipped on some grease in the kitchen and fell, breaking her hip in two places. After she recovered, she pleaded with my mother to take her back, convinced that the accident was "God's punishment" for her disloyalty. The broken hip left her with a permanent limp, and she was forced to move down to a room in the cellar near the oil burner where it was warm and dry. The slightest change in weather caused her pain, but she accepted it as part of her "punishment."

Aside from her hip and her other endless complaints (backaches, headaches, stomachaches, all loudly attributed to my brother and me), she grew almost deaf. She rarely heard the phone when it rang, and when she did she would pick up the receiver, bellow "Iss nobody home!" and slam it down again. She seldom answered doorbells. And for protection Meta was better than the FBI, Scotland Yard and Brinks all rolled into one. Doors, windows, everything was bolted and chained at least two or three times. As she grew older, she couldn't even hear us pounding on the door. Then my father would have to run around the side of the porch, crawl through the bushes and rap on the cellar window. Even then he wasn't always successful. Once we stood outside in a blinding snowstorm for half an hour, trying to get into our own house!

Meta disapproved of smoking, drinking, and most of all, my brother's parties. When he was in college, he would often bring friends home with him for the weekend. If my parents happened to be in the country, Meta would race around the house gathering up all the glasses and ashtrays and beer, hiding them in remote places, all in the vain hope of discouraging a party. Naturally this led to arguments, lectures, dire threats, but in the end she always relented and reluctantly carried them back again.

"Ach, de drinkin' and de smokin' and de yellin'—vat I haff suffered here!" she would complain to anyone who would listen.

"I Go in April." Deep down in the mysterious recesses of her room Meta kept an enormous trunk which was locked, double-locked and firmly guarded from all eyes. No one had ever seen its contents, not even my mother. And every year, she threatened to pack up all her things and move back to "Chermany." This went on from the time I was four until I passed my 26th birthday. She was going to buy her ticket and leave in April because we were too much trouble, she was getting old, the food was fresher in Germany, and so forth. But when April approached she would give no sign of leaving.

"I go in July," she would say. "April iss too colt."

July was too hot. "I go in October, ven it isn't so crowded."

In October the holidays were coming up, and she felt she ought to stay at least until after New Year's.

In January "der iss too much snow"—and so it was back to April and the whole cycle began over again.

Once, after a disagreement with my mother, she actually went down to the Passport Bureau, but "der vass such a long line, mitt mine hip I couldn't vait..." And so she stayed on, growing frailer and older and grumpier every year, still planning to leave in April.

Just as Meta didn't believe in telling tales behind people's backs, she didn't believe in complimenting them to their faces either. It came as a shock to us when we heard, through others, that Meta took any pride in us at all. But our graduation from college, my brother's final discharge from the Army (although she greeted him at the door with a gruff, "Vat—*you* again?"), his choice of a bride, all filled her with a special delight. To others she worried about us constantly: I wasn't eating enough at school, Ed's wife wouldn't feed him the things he liked.

"I vunder if dat girl knows how to cook," she would mutter. "I t'ink maybe I go to der apartment and giff dem a goot meal."

When I got married ("Ach, *finally!*" was her comment), she offered to come and take care of us.

"But Meta," I said, touched and embarrassed at the same time. "I'd love it but...well, you see, we haven't much money."

"I don't vant any money," she said, deeply offended.

"But we only have a small apartment. There wouldn't be any room for you." I saw the expression on her face, and tried hastily to explain: "But maybe later on, when we can afford a bigger apartment..."

Her face brightened. "All right, den. Maybe later. You vill see—it isn't so easy to take care of a house by yourself. I come and giff you goot meals."

Like Hoarded Jewels. Alas, Meta never even saw our apartment. That summer, she finally took that trip back to Germany to visit her nieces and nephews, some of whom she'd never met. While there, she became ill and died. When the news came, my brother and I were stunned. Not Meta. Our Meta was indestructible. Meta was always there. The seasons might change, we might grow up and get married and have children, but Meta went on forever. I couldn't believe that a part of my life had been swept away, in a distant country, without any of us there to tell her how much we missed her and wanted her to get well.

When my mother and I could gather the courage to do it, we went down to Meta's room and sadly put away her things, sensing her presence more strongly than ever, acutely aware of the hole she had left in our lives. The trunk which she had fiercely protected from us all stood silent in the corner. For some strange reason it wasn't locked.

I had always wanted to know the contents of that trunk, but now I approached it with grave reluctance. We opened the lid to see if there was anything we could send to her family. But all we found were mementos of us.

Pictures of my brother and me at various ages, part of my old jump rope, our engagement and marriage announcements, one of Gigi's dog collars. Every gift we had given her over the years was carefully wrapped in tissue paper, tied up with the original ribbon. As we went through each layer of our lives, memories came drifting back to me in vivid detail—small, forgotten things which Meta had lovingly preserved as if they were jewels. When we finally came to the bottom, there was an old leather pouch with a drawstring, so heavy we could barely lift it out.

There was a note pinned to the side. "To Eddie and Karol," it said simply. "I leev all mine money. Meta."

Inside was over $6000 which she had meticulously saved, coin by coin, over the past 40 years. Every quarter, every dollar, including the gifts of money which we had given her at Christmas and birthdays, still folded inside the original cards. There was a long silence. I looked at my mother and, in a voice that cracked, I said the only thing I could think of to say at the moment.

"Oh, Meta. You never could spell my name right. . . ."

And then I broke down and wept, unashamed.

My Impractical Wife, Signe

by Kavanaugh MacDonald

Had I taken Signe to a marriage counselor when she first got it into her pretty head I was the man heaven intended for her, I am sure I would have learned that she was *not* designed for a job as serious as matrimony. But our courtship was such a deliriously impractical affair that we never sought advice, and it is my good fortune we didn't.

Not that Signe has changed. She still can't cook. She can't, or won't, keep house. She can't add—and will forever believe that all there is to household financing is the down payment.

Yet Signe and I have been married for nearly ten years, and I cannot imagine a more satisfying marriage. We have a home which, though modest, is one of the merriest in the neighborhood. We have three lovely and uncomplicated children. And our adventures have been such that when I sat down to think them over tonight my eyes began to mist.

Is she so very beautiful then? Yes, she is. But it would take more than her dark-blonde hair, her lovely figure and country-fresh beauty to make me forgive the chronic disorder of her house and her way of life. When I come home from work I can be fairly certain there will be a pile of dust at the head of the stairs where the sweeping was not finished. There will be dishes in the kitchen sink, a loaf of bread that has been left open-ended all day, and so on and on.

I have argued fruitlessly about these things many times—and about the clutter in our living room. Signe collects almost everything that doesn't cost money: rocks, butterflies, wild-flowers, birds' eggs and heaven knows what else. These collections adorn the bookshelves, the piano, the living-room table. I have never met anyone else to whom souvenirs mean so much. Every trip we have made, every year of each baby's life, every household event of any importance must have its souvenir, and that souvenir must be in the living room.

I once suggested she take a few bushels of these things to the attic. She said, "But why have souvenirs if they aren't where they can remind you?" For that I had no answer, and the collecting goes on.

In our first years together, when I came home and found the house looking like Tokyo after an earthquake, I would explode with indignation. Signe would listen with such apparent contrition that she would have me almost persuaded. Then she would venture her excuse: she and the children had gone swimming, or gathering wild strawberries, or to the woods for trilliums. Her excuses never bore any resemblance to an argument—Signe never argues. On those earlier occasions I invariably ended the session as embarrassed as a hound encountering a rabbit that will not run.

I have not entirely given up on the housekeeping lectures, but now my efforts spring from habit rather than hope. "Suppose my boss or the school principal or the minister should drop in on us now," I say. "How would you feel?"

It is a foolish question. These three and countless other people of our town drop in at our house almost constantly—because they like it. They enter without invitation (preceded by only the faintest formality of knocking), throw the accumulation of toys or children's coats or magazines from the chairs, and stretch out their legs as if they were on a park bench in Florida.

There is the old bachelor from two streets away who is forever bringing us fish. Signe set aside a corner of the freezer for his use. But the best fish, he always insists, are for her.

There is Mrs. Mercer, the little old lady who had to move to a small apartment in which she could not keep her Persian cat and springer dog. Signe found her crying because she had to part with them. The animals have been at our place ever since—and Mrs. Mercer with them a good bit of the time.

Then there is Mr. Powley, who brings the comics every Sunday morning and reads them to our children. He gets in the way when we are rushing to get the children scrubbed for Sunday school and his cigar is strong enough to mothproof the room, but Signe is always delighted when he comes. "He likes children," she explains. "He had two boys of his own, and lost them in the war."

There are others. The breadman who drops around with his family of an evening; the excitable little woman who comes every time she has a squabble with her husband. The list could go on and on.

To Signe, everyone means well. Evil is something she has yet to meet, apparently. Last winter she bought some plastic dishes from an enthusiastic door-to-door salesman. A week later I saw the same brand of dishes in a downtown store for two-thirds the price. "Those at the store must be seconds or thinner or something," said Signe. "That man at the door wouldn't have charged me more for the same thing!"

Even if I had proved to her the two sets were identical, I'm sure she would have suggested that the man got his prices mixed up. It would be beyond her belief that anyone might want to take advantage of her.

And that includes the army. It was the Canadian Army that brought on our one big quarrel—and in me produced a great awakening.

We live on the edge of a Canadian town and a neck of the army proving ground comes within a stone's throw of our back yard. This camp had been here for years without giving us cause to notice it. So I was surprised one hot August evening when I came home from the office and found an ack-ack gun on a jeep staring me in the face. The captain who was driving the jeep said casually, "Hot night, isn't it?"

I agreed, whereupon he said good night and drove back to camp.

I asked Signe to explain. "They were having maneuvers," she told me, "and it was so hot I thought they'd like some cold buttermilk." She laughed. "The eight of them drank six quarts!"

"Six quarts!" I spluttered.

Her face fell. "But I didn't buy it out of the grocery money, darling," she explained. "I took it out of the ginger pot."

That was the place where for two years Signe had been stowing away driblets of cash for the playroom she always wanted us to build.

"Look, dear," I said, "you've got to consider your reputation. If some of these old women around here find out you're playing host to the army, what will they say?"

She didn't make up tales about other women, she said, so how could she know that other women might be eager to do that about her? "I saved some buttermilk for you," she added. "It's awfully good." That was the end of my sermon.

There was no ack-ack gun in my lane the next afternoon, nor any soldiers. But there were six empty buttermilk bottles on the sink.

"They bought it themselves this time," Signe told me blithely. "They're very nice boys."

"That captain especially," I said.

"He is," she said. "He's been in Korea, you know."

The third night there were eight buttermilk bottles, and I got ready to lay down the law, but just then the captain came. How would we like to come over to the camp movies tonight? he asked. Bring the whole family.

It's hard to tell a man off when he's so genial. Besides, Signe was already starting to scrub the children's elbows for the event.

I have to admit I didn't have a bad time that night.

Two nights later the captain and a couple of his boys brought the movie machine over and put on a show for the whole neighborhood on our lawn. A few nights after that he brought over a Highlander, kilt, pipes and all, and paraded him up and down the lawn to the delight of Mrs. Mercer, Mr. Powley and a dozen others. In short, the captain had become one of the club.

While I could never quite seem to find the way to say so, I didn't like it. The captain and his boys would come at the slightest excuse: to borrow a pen, to borrow a record, to lend a record, to get darning thread or a needle. They mowed the lawn, took Mrs. Mercer's springer out for exercise, baby-sat, trimmed the lilacs.

"Do you realize how little privacy we have now?" I asked Signe one night. "It's your fault—you make them feel so damned welcome!"

"But they're lonely," she said.

About a month later we came to the parting of the ways. My work had taken me out of town for a couple of days, and when I got home I scarcely recognized the place. The whole back porch had been remodeled, extended and covered. It was the playroom.

Signe threw her arms about me. "The army boys did it for me!" she said. "The captain got the plywood from some wreckers. All I had to buy was the two-by-fours and tarpaper!"

The scene that followed is something I'd rather not recall. Whose home was this anyhow? I demanded. Why wasn't I consulted? Suppose I couldn't afford the job just then—why should she advertise my poverty? Besides, who wanted tarpaper? I had always wanted shingles.

I didn't eat dinner at home that night. I went downtown to cool off.

When I came back three hours later the house was empty. All the privacy a man could ask for—and the most desolate house I had ever seen. There was a note saying the children were with Mrs. Mercer. No hint as to Signe's whereabouts.

I walked around the house trying to find relief by noticing all the things that were out of place or untidy. It didn't help much. "She'll be over at the camp," I told myself. "Saturday-night dance." So I went over to the camp recreation hall.

She was there all right, and she was dancing. I sat down at a table in a corner and waited.

The captain must have been watching for me, because he came to my table almost at once. "I was waiting for you," he said.

He took out a cigarette and looked at it a long time. "So

you're sore. I'm sorry I didn't see that we were getting on your nerves."

"I came to take my wife home," I burst out.

"Look," said the captain, "you're one of the damnedest fools I've ever met! I'm sorry you didn't like the playroom. My boys chipped in several bucks apiece for that plywood, and four of them gave up a trip home to help put the room up. Signe wanted to surprise you, and we wanted to do what would make her happy. Do you think there was something else we had in our filthy minds?"

I didn't answer.

"Look at the men here," he went on. "They've been all over the world, and have seen every mean, ugly thing there is. Some of them have spent half a lifetime doing their bit to straighten out the mess some stinker's meanness has caused. And then one day they run across somebody that hasn't an ounce of selfishness. And a bunch of swell kids. Is it any wonder they like to hang around your place?

"Give us a world full of people like that woman and you could plow up every damned army camp in the world and put in potatoes! You're the man that's got her, and you're belly-aching about it! I know it's tough having to share her, but you can't keep a woman like that entirely to yourself any more than you can copyright a hunk of sunbeam!"

Somehow I had forgotten my wrath. I merely looked across the floor at Signe and started for the door.

The captain said, "Don't worry about her. Go home and think over what I've told you. I'll bring her home. She's not happy here tonight, anyhow."

So I went home to think it over and to take another lonely walk around the house looking at all the junk, the rocks, the plastic dishes. What was all this disorder? I asked myself. Perhaps it was only evidence of one so wholeheartedly absorbed in a life that was full and good and interesting she simply hadn't time to bother filing the pieces of it into pigeonholes.

The captain brought Signe back about midnight. As he had observed, she wasn't happy. She wasn't happy until I finally got up enough courage to apologize. Then, once again, she became the woman everybody loved.

The captain returned the following Monday to see how we were getting along. In the late afternoon next day he brought the buttermilk boys over to finish the playroom, while the Highlander paraded in the back yard with his pipes screaming triumph.

Courage, and Farewell

by Romain Gary

The day war was declared my mother drove five hours in a taxi to say good-by and to wish me, in her own words, "A hundred victories in the sky." I was at that time gunnery instructor at the air force academy in Salon-de-Provence in the south of France.

I saw her step down from the ancient, flat-nosed Renault, leaning on her cane, a cigarette in the corner of her mouth, under the interested eyes of the assembled soldiery.

I walked over to her slowly, thoroughly embarrassed by this intrusion of a mother into the virile world in which I enjoyed a hard-won reputation as a tough and even a slightly dangerous, devil-may-care character. In a voice loud enough for all to hear, she announced:

"You will be a second Guynemer! Your mother has always been right!"

I could hear the roar of laughter behind my back. She

grabbed her cane and, with a threatening gesture toward the mocking audience, delivered another inspired prophecy:

"You will be a great hero, a general, ambassador of France! This rabble doesn't know who you are!"

When I tried, in a furious whisper, to tell her she was ruining me in the eyes of our air force, her lips began to tremble, a hurt look came into her eyes: "You are ashamed of your old mother!"

That did it: all the trappings of laboriously assumed toughness collapsed. I put an arm around her shoulders and held her tight. I no longer heard the laughter. We were back once more, the two of us, in a magical world, born out of a mother's murmur into a child's ear, a promise whispered at dawn of future triumphs and greatness, of justice and love. I looked confidently at the sky, so empty and thus so open to my future deeds; I was thinking of the day when I should return to her victorious, having given a meaning to her life of self-denial and sacrifice.

I was 13 years old and we were living in Nice. Each morning I went to school, leaving my mother at the hotel where she rented a showcase, displaying on its shelves a few *articles de luxe* borrowed from the local shops. On each scarf, belt, clip or sweater sold she received a commission of ten percent. Except for a two-hour break at noon when I came home for lunch, she sat there all day long, keeping her eyes open for prospective clients. Our survival depended entirely upon this humble and precarious business.

Exiled from her native Russia, alone, without husband or friends, for more than ten years she had been putting up a brave fight to keep us going, to pay for bread and butter and rent, school fees, clothes, shoes and, above all, to achieve that daily miracle, the beefsteak which she set before me for lunch, with a proud and happy smile, as though it were the very symbol of her victorious struggle against adversity.

She never touched any of the meat herself, maintaining that her diet forbade animal fats. Then one day, leaving the table, I went into the kitchen for a glass of water. My mother was seated on a stool, holding the frying pan on her knees. She was carefully sopping up with small chunks of bread the fat in which my steak had been cooked, and then eating the bread with obvious relish. When she saw me, she quickly tried to hide the pan under a napkin, but it was too late: the true reason for her vegetarian diet was now obvious to me.

My mother was always in a hurry for me to "become someone." Despite my many failures, she always believed in me. "And how are things at school?" she would ask.

"I got another zero in math."

My mother would think this over.

"Your teachers don't understand you," she would say firmly. "They'll be sorry one day. The time will come when your name will be inscribed in letters of gold on the wall of their wretched school. I'll go and tell them so tomorrow. I'll read your latest poems to them. You will be a d'Annunzio, a Victor Hugo. They don't know who you are!"

Often, when she had come back from her work my mother would sit down, light a cigarette, cross her legs and look at me with a knowing smile. Then her eyes would be fixed over my shoulder on some mysterious, bright point in our future, visible only to her in the magical land where all the beauty lies.

"You are going to be a French ambassador," she would say, or rather state, with absolute conviction. I had not the slightest idea what the phrase meant.

"Good," I would say with a nonchalant air.

"You will have a motorcar."

She had not had enough to eat and she had walked home with the temperature well below freezing.

"All it will take is a little patience."

When I was 16 my mother became manageress of the Hôtel-Pension Mermonts in Nice. She got up at six every morning, drank a cup of tea, took her cane and went to the Buffa Market. She always returned home with a load of fruit and flowers. Then she would go down to the kitchens, draw up the menu, see the tradespeople, inspect the cellar, do her accounts and attend to every detail of the business.

One day, after going up and down the accursed stairs from the restaurant to the kitchens, which she climbed at least 20 times a day, she suddenly collapsed into a chair. Her face and lips were gray. We were lucky to get a doctor quickly, and his diagnosis was rapid. She had given herself too much insulin. It was thus I learned what she had been concealing from me for years: she was a diabetic and each morning gave herself an injection of insulin before starting on the day's work.

I was in a state of abject terror. The memory of her gray face, of her head leaning slightly sideways, of her hand clutching painfully at her breast, never again left me. The idea that she might die before I had done all that she expected of me, that she might leave this world without ever having known *justice*, seemed to me to be a denial of the most elementary common sense, of good manners and law.

The legend of my future was what was keeping her alive. I could only swallow my shame and continue my race against time in an attempt to give to an absurd, fond dream at least some small core of reality.

I was inducted into the air force in 1938. When war was declared, my mother came to say good-by to me in that Renault taxi. Leaning on her stick that day she solemnly inspected our aviation strength.

"All the machines have open cockpits," she remarked. "Remember that you have a delicate throat."

I could not resist pointing out that if all the Luftwaffe was going to give me was a sore throat, I would consider myself very lucky. She smiled and gave me a superior, almost ironical look. "Nothing is going to happen to you," she told me, with perfect tranquillity.

Her face expressed complete confidence. It was as though she *knew*, as though she had made a pact with Fate, as though in exchange for her own botched life she had been given certain guarantees, received certain promises.

"No, nothing will happen to me, Mother. I promise you that."

She hesitated. Some struggle was going on inside her and it was reflected in her face. Then she made a little concession. "You may, perhaps, be wounded in the leg," she said.

A few weeks before the German offensive, a telegram came: *Mother seriously ill, come at once.*

I arrived at Nice very early in the morning, and went to the Saint-Antoine clinic. My mother's head was deeply sunk in the pillow. Her cheeks were hollow; her face bore a troubled, worried air. On the bedside table was the silver medal which

I had won at the ping-pong championship of Nice in 1932.

"You need a woman by your side," she told me.

I said something like: "All men do."

"Yes," she said. "But it'll be more difficult for you than for others. It's my fault."

We played cards. She looked at me from time to time with a concentrated attention, a cunning and calculating air, and I knew that she was cooking up something once more. But I was very far from suspecting what she had in mind. I am convinced that her little scheme first entered her head then.

My leave came to an end. I don't know how to describe that parting. There are no words. But I put on a good face. I didn't cry or anything—I remembered what she had told me.

"Well, so long." I kissed her cheek with a smile. What that smile cost me only she could know, because she, too, smiled:

"Don't worry about me. I'm an old warhorse. I've kept going till now and I can carry on for a bit longer. Take off your cap."

I took it off. She made the sign of the cross on my forehead with her finger. "I give you my blessing."

I went to the door. We looked at each other once more; we were both smiling. I felt quite calm. Something of her courage had passed into me and it has remained with me ever since. Her courage and her will continue to burn in me even now.

After the fall of France I was lent to the RAF, and my mother's first letters reached me shortly after my arrival in England. They were sent secretly to a friend in Switzerland, and then forwarded to London, "Care of General de Gaulle."

Until my return to Nice, three years and six months later, until the very eve of victory, these letters, dateless and timeless, as though coming out of eternity, were to follow me faithfully in all my wanderings. For three and a half years her breath breathed life into me, and I was sustained by a will stronger than my own: the umbilical cord fed my blood with the fighting courage of a heart more gallant than mine.

"My glorious and beloved son," she would write. *"We read in the papers, with feelings of gratitude and admiration, the tales of your exploits. In the sky of Cologne, of Hamburg, of Bremen, your outspread wings fill enemy hearts with terror."*

I found no difficulty in understanding what was going on in her mind. Whenever the RAF raided a target, I was one of those engaged. In each burst of a bomb she recognized my voice. I was present on every front and made the enemy tremble, and each time a German aircraft was brought down by English fighters it was to me, quite naturally, that she credited the victory. The alleys of the Buffa Market resounded with the echo of my deeds. After all, she knew me: she knew that it was I who had won the ping-pong championship of Nice in 1932.

Her letters were becoming shorter, mere pencil scribbles written in a hurry. They reached me four or five at a time. She was well. She was receiving the insulin regularly. *"My glorious son, I am proud of you. . . . Vive la France!"* There seemed to be no trace of anxiety, but there was a new note of sadness in her latest letters: *"Dear son, I beg you not to think of me, not to be fearful on my account. Have courage. Remember that you no longer need me, that you are a man now, that you can stand on your own feet. Get married soon. Don't think too much about me. My health is good. Old Dr. Rosanoff is very pleased with me. He sends you his best wishes. Be strong, I beg you; be brave. Your mother."*

My heart was heavy. Something was wrong, something in that letter remained unsaid. But what really mattered was that she was still alive, and my hope of winning my race against time and returning home triumphant grew stronger with each day that passed.

After the Allied landings, I sensed in the letters reaching me from Nice a feeling of joy and serenity as though my mother knew at last that the goal was in sight. There was about them an especial note of tenderness and also of apology for which I could not altogether account.

"My beloved son, we have been separated now for many years and I hope that you have grown accustomed to my absence since, after all, I am not on this earth forever. Remember that I have never had a shadow of doubt about you. I do hope that when you come back and understand everything, you will forgive me. I could not have acted otherwise."

What was it she had done that needed my forgiveness? I racked my brains, but to no purpose.

Paris was now on the point of being liberated, and I arranged to have myself parachuted into the south of France for liaison duties with the Resistance. I was in a hurry—my blood boiled with impatience, and nothing mattered to me now except getting back to her. Then the Allied landings in the south of France cut short my parachuting plans. So I arranged immediately for a "special mission order."

Now I was coming home, with the green-and-black ribbon of the Cross of the Liberation prominently displayed upon my chest, above the Croix de Guerre and five or six other medals of which I had forgotten none, with my officer's stripes on the shoulders of my black battle dress, my cap tilted over one eye and with a more than usually tough expression, owing to my facial paralysis. I had written a novel, and I carried its French and English editions in my shoulder bag. There was just enough lead in my body to give it some weight. I was intoxicated with hope, youth, certainty.

It is painful for me to continue my story, and I will do so as rapidly as possible. At our Hôtel-Pension Mermonts there was no one to greet me. Those I questioned remembered vaguely having heard of a strange old Russian lady who ran the place years ago, but they had not met her. My mother had died three years and six months earlier! But she had known that I would never be able to stand on my own feet and fight as befits a Frenchman unless she was there to give me her support; and she had made her plans accordingly.

During the last few days before her death, she wrote nearly 250 letters and sent them to her friend in Switzerland. The undated letters were to be forwarded to me at regular intervals. This was, no doubt, what she was scheming with so much love when I caught that naïve and cunning expression in her eyes, when we parted for the last time at the Saint-Antoine clinic.

And so I had gone on receiving from my mother the strength and the courage I so greatly needed to carry me through to the day of victory, when she had been dead for more than three years.

"So You're Kate's Girl!"

by Jeanmarie Coogan

My mother couldn't stand me when I was little, and I couldn't stand her. Neither of us was what the other would have chosen for a life companion.

The mother I had in mind for myself was middle-aged with brown hair pulled back in a bun. She wore an apron, baked a lot, was serious and soft-spoken, and sang hymns. Before her marriage she had been a schoolteacher or librarian.

My real mother had quit school to go to work and help out at home. She was 19 when I was born, a tall tomboy with flyaway blonde hair and the wide shoulders, narrow hips and long legs of an athlete—which she was. Her temperament was strictly Irish. In the grimmest circumstances my mother could always find a bit of fun, and she had a great shout of a laugh that exploded like firecrackers. An invalid neighbor often told me, "I love to hear your mother laugh." That neighbor lived two houses away. Other mothers called their children home in a shaky soprano. My mother put two fingers to her lips and produced a whistle that could be heard in the next block.

My mother's idea of a good time was to crowd a lot of people (preferably relatives, of whom we had thousands) into our small house, provide drinks and cold cuts, dancing in the early part of the evening, singing toward the end, and fun and jokes all night long. Far from being a hymn singer, she lullabied me with "Melancholy Baby." As for my father, he seemed to think everything about her was just great.

If my mother wasn't what I had in mind, I was even farther from her beau ideal. I wasn't even the right sex. When I was born, she was so incredulous to find I wasn't a boy that she had to ask her sister to think up a name for me. She soon decided, however, that I was the biggest, fattest baby in the hospital nursery and therefore worthwhile.

And besides, having come from a family of ten, she anticipated other opportunities to use all those good boys' names she had thought of. Then, one year after I was born, an emergency operation destroyed the possibility of her ever having another child. This explains a lot to me now, but all I knew then was that it was hard enough to be one child to my mother, and I just wasn't up to being ten.

Take spunk. Spunk was very big with my mother. When I would come in crying because someone had hit me, she would say, "Look, put up your fists like this."

"I can't!" I'd wail.

"Put up your fists," she'd command. I'd just wail louder. Then she would cock her right, ready to land one on *me* out of sheer despair.

My mother decided that I was to be a beautiful, talented, rich singing-and-dancing child movie star. With spunk. So, at three I was enrolled in Miss La Palme's School of the Dance: toe, tap, ballet and acrobatics. At four, I was doing so well that Miss La Palme used me for demonstrations. This was a good time for my mother, and she was busy taking me to lessons, parish hall shows, women's-club recitals and talent nights at local theaters.

But all this came to an early end. In first grade I learned to read. It was a heady experience, the key to a magic door. From the school reader I went on to reading cereal boxes, advertisements on the trolley, medicine-bottle labels. A pattern emerged: "What do you mean, 'Just as soon as I finish this page'? You practice that new routine *now*." Then, "I'm sick of having you hang around that library."

Finally my mother came upon me, the night before a recital, reading instead of rehearsing. "Dear God," she cried, calling on Highest Authority to witness, "reading! Sitting there reading! And that Shirley Temple out there making a mint!" Tears filled her eyes, and she turned away.

At last the ultimatum: "Reading, or dancing lessons. What's it going to be?" Her face showed hurt, despair and puzzlement when I said, "Reading."

That weekend she told Aunt Margaret, who said, "Maybe it's for the best, Kate. I mean, look at her. She's almost seven, kind of string-beany, two front teeth missing. She's no Shirley Temple."

"All right," my mother shot back, "but she *could* be Jane Withers."

As I grew older, our scenes with shouting and crying on both sides became fewer. By high school Mother and I were even beginning to understand each other—a little.

Athletics were always important in her family. In the early 1920s, when she was growing up in Philadelphia, her brother Tod played with the Phillies a while, and all nine others in the family—boys and girls—played for various semipro baseball, football, basketball and softball teams. For several years, my mother and her sister had dominated the scoring columns in the women's sport leagues. Whenever we were out with her family, some stranger was sure to come over and ask one of them, "Say, isn't your name Dennehey? I remember seeing you play . . ."

I went to an all-girls high school, and my mother was pleased when I made the varsity basketball team but dismayed to learn I was a guard.

"When are you going to play forward?" she asked.

I answered, "Never."

"But, Jeanmarie, you'll never get to score!" She never enjoyed the game quite as much after that.

In another thing I was beginning to meet her standards: spunk. When I graduated from high school I won a partial scholarship to college. College had never once crossed her mind. My father was in the Army then, and my mother, to supplement the allotment, worked as a stitcher in a book-bindery for $24 a week. Even with my summer and afterschool jobs, we were just barely making it. When I told her the news, she was speechless.

But one day shortly afterward she announced proudly, "Jeanmarie, you *are* going to college." She had got a job paying $60 a week, a phenomenal sum those days, cleaning cars on the Pennsylvania Railroad. It was a dirty, back-breaking man's job, but she never complained. Partly because I didn't know what hard physical labor was, partly because of her own attitude, I never questioned that my mother should work so hard for my dream.

In college I made honors in my studies. But this didn't please my mother so much as when I was chosen to attend various student conventions—all expenses paid. My mother had been as far as Atlantic City a few times, and it seemed very glamorous to her that I should be going to New York or Chicago. It seemed glamorous to me, too. I would board the train wearing a classmate's fur jacket, another friend's skirt, and looking like one of those all-American girls who pose for soft-drink ads—the kind of girl who had the Sunday New York *Times* delivered at home, a girl with a mild, soft-spoken mother who before marriage had been a schoolteacher or librarian. That's how I looked.

One day when I announced a trip, my mother said she would be working in the yards at the time my train would be leaving and she would wave. When the train pulled out I scanned the railroad yard, and finally I could make out a figure waving. It was my mother. I stood up and waved vigorously. But the sun was in her eyes and, unable to see, she just kept waving her hand slowly back and forth. I saw her: blonde hair pulled back in a bandanna, thick-soled shoes, work-hardened hands. In my borrowed finery, standing on the floor that could have been scrubbed by my mother—all of a sudden it seemed terribly important that she see me and know I was answering her. I waved and waved, but the small figure just kept waving unseeingly until we were out of sight.

The Irish code of conduct permits one to be flamboyantly emotional in public, but in private one's deepest feelings are held in strict reserve. Yet I know that day I could openly have told my mother how much I loved her.

The chance never came again. She died a few years after I graduated from college. Between my growing up and her death, however, I came to know it can be a joy to live with someone who is completely different from you. We could never say the words, but my mother knew how I felt about her; I knew how she felt about me.

A few months after her death I was at a convention when a stranger came up to me. "This may sound crazy," he said, "but is your name Dennehey?"

"No, but my mother's was," I answered.

He snapped his fingers. "So you're Kate's girl! I haven't seen her since she was a kid. I used to play ball with Tod— I knew all the Denneheys. Great people." He shook his head, smiling. "You're Kate Dennehey's girl, all right. I'd know you anywhere."

I laughed and said, "Thank you. That's the nicest thing that's ever been said to me." And I meant it with all my heart.

In the Spotlight

"Satchmo"—Greatest Jazz Musician of All

by Tyree Glenn

My, how he could blow that horn! He'd mop his glistening brow with a white handkerchief, put that big golden trumpet to his lips, point it heavenward and blow, and the notes would pour out pretty as smoke rings. And when he growled a song, in that gravel voice, flashing those big, pearly teeth, bouncing and jiving, well, there just wasn't anyone like him in the world. If you were a musician and ever played with Louis Armstrong, or even heard him play, there was always a little of Satchmo in your music ever after. "The Reverend Satchelmouth," Bing Crosby once said, "is the beginning and the end of music in America."

Before "Pops," as most of his friends called him, came to the rowdy Chicago of the 1920s, jazz was usually performed in ensemble. But young Louis, by the sheer virtuosity of his skill, soon began freeing the music for the individual performer. Under his influence, the whole makeup of jazz was changed and broadened. It became a unique American art form, and he became one of its biggest stars. He traveled all over the world and was as popular abroad as at home. He appeared in 36 movies, was a top television attraction and made some 2500 records, including such lasting hits as "Mack the Knife," "Hello, Dolly!" "Blueberry Hill" and "When It's Sleepy Time Down South."

Yet it was not as a musician and entertainer that Louis left his most lasting mark, but rather as a rare human being who won love by giving it. His philosophy was: "If you don't treat me right, shame on you." He overcame poverty and the slights and cruelties of racial bigotry and never let them scar him. He was just too good and gentle a man, too full of fun and small jokes, to carry a grudge. "He even wakes up smiling," his wife, Lucille, said.

I first heard Louis' distinctive sound on records when I was a kid out of Corsicana, Texas, playing trombone with a band. Those jubilant trumpet notes, pure and brilliant, and that gravelly voice, just knocked out our whole outfit. We used to ride along sticking our heads out of the bus so we could catch cold and sing like Louis Armstrong. But no one ever succeeded. A few years later, when I came to New York to back up Ethel Waters at the Cotton Club, I got to sit in on some jam sessions with Louis. I was in seventh heaven. Finally, when he asked me to join his band, I had the great experience of playing and traveling all over the world with him.

It was a lesson not merely in music but in living. Playing in a band, doing one-night stands, getting too little sleep and bad food, is a tough grind, but Pops had a knack of taking it all in stride. He could curl up and catnap almost anywhere. "I don't like nothing to fret me," he would say. "You healthier and happier when you hang loose."

Always Reaching. Louis was born July 4, 1900, in the poor black "Back o' Town" section of New Orleans. He grew up in a world of bordellos, gamblers, Creole culture, razor fights and jazz. His mother, whom he adored, was a domestic, and his father, a turpentine worker, soon deserted them. "My mama taught me that anything you can't get—to hell with it," he used to recall. Little Louis scrounged out a meager living delivering coal to sporting houses, and it was there he heard his first jazz: great musicians like Jelly Roll Morton, Bunk Johnson and Joe "King" Oliver.

When he was 13, in a burst of youthful exuberance, Louis shot off some blank cartridges to celebrate New Year's Eve. He was sent to the Colored Waifs Home. This proved a blessing in disguise, for there he was taught to play the bugle and cornet. After he got out, his idol, King Oliver, gave him an old cornet and taught him more about playing it. Louis did a stint playing on riverboats out of New Orleans and St. Louis, and then Oliver summoned him to join his band in Chicago. "I was just a kid at the time," Louis would recall. "Didn't know nothing. Didn't even *suspect* much."

Before long, though, "Little Louis" (he was a roly-poly 225 pounds) was making the other musicians take notice with his prodigious blowing. He had the ideal equipment for a great horn player: barrel chest, powerful diaphragm and the full lips and mouth which earned him the nickname "Satchelmouth" (eventually shortened to "Satchmo"). So powerful was his blowing that when the Oliver band made records, sound engineers had to place Satchmo 20 feet behind the other musicians to balance his part with the rest of the band.

But Louis could do more than just blow with incredible power. He was always reaching out, trying new sounds, new ideas: "We all go *do, re, mi,*" he would say, "but you got to find the other notes for yourself." Louis found them in his own eventful life. "When I blow I think of times from outa the past that give me an image," he once told writer Larry King. "A town, a chick somewhere back down the line, an old man with no name you once seen in a place you don't remember. What you hear coming from a man's horn, that's what he is."

In 1924, Louis went to New York to join the orchestra of Fletcher Henderson, the first big black band. At an early rehearsal, he blew with customary power, tossing off high C's like confetti. Henderson, a highly trained musician, asked Louis if he had seen the letters "pp," for *pianissimo*, or "play very softly." Louis laughed and said, "I thought 'pp' meant 'pound plenty.'" Henderson gave Louis his head, and soon his playing changed the Henderson band from a dance orchestra into the first real jazz band.

Dark Side. As Louis' popularity soared, he became a business in himself. In 1932, he made his first of many trips abroad, pulling enormous crowds wherever he played. Pops used to enjoy telling me about his trips before I joined the band. "We drew 120,000 people in the Congo," he once recalled. "Fifty of those cats brought me to this big king. The king takes one look and yells out, 'Satchmo!' Well, I yell right back, 'Whattaya say, king!'" Once, in Rome, Louis and his wife had an audience with Pope Pius XII. The Pope asked the Armstrongs if they had any children. "Not yet," Louis said, "but we're trying." "Well," the Pope replied, "I'll pray for you."

While acclaimed by kings and notables abroad, Louis experienced the dark side of America on his endless one-night stands in the South in the 1930s and '40s. He and his musicians traveled in a big Packard and sometimes slept in the car by the side of the road because white hotels wouldn't accept black people. "I played a jillion hotels I couldn't stay at," Pops used to recall in his rare glum moments. "But later, after I'd made my reputation, I had them put it in my contract that I wouldn't play in no place I couldn't stay. I was the first Negro in the business to crack them big white hotels."

Despite such treatment, Louis remained philosophical. Once he was sitting in his dressing room when pianist Errol Garner came by. "Hi, Pops," Garner said. "What's new?" Louis looked up and smiled wanly. "White folks still in the lead," he said. Still, Louis could get mad. He canceled a scheduled tour of the Soviet Union for the State Department because of resistance to school integration in Little Rock, Ark. "When I see on television a crowd of whites spitting at a little colored girl, I think I have a right to get sore," he fumed. "After all, America is my country, too."

Softest Touch. For all his wealth and fame, Louis remained a simple man. "I never did want to be no big star," he used to say. "All this traveling around, all *grandioso*, it's nice, but I didn't suggest it. I was just as happy in New Orleans." He lived simply in an old 11-room house in a quiet New York neighborhood with his wife, Lucille. His favorite dish was red beans and rice. He loved the neighborhood kids, and they adored him. Many's the time our band bus arrived to pick up

Louis at his house, only to have to wait while he bought ice cream for the kids.

Pops was the softest touch in the world and used to drive Joe Glaser (his white business manager) crazy with his generosity. "Pops actually gives away—I mean *gives* away—$500 to $1000 every damn week," Glaser once exploded. "I don't mean every month. I mean every damn *week*." Several times I saw him give away his trumpet to some kid who couldn't afford one.

Louis was, as he said, "one of those hy-po-CHON-dree-acs." Before each show he had a ritual of treating himself with various nostrums. There was a swallow of honey and glycerine to "wash out the pipes" and a lip salve from Germany to "take care of the chops." There was a liniment to be smeared on throat, chest and stomach to ward off colds, and sweet spirits of niter daubed on his face "to take away the fever." Finally, there was his nightly dose of Swiss Kriss, a physic which was almost a mania with him. It was funny to see Pops, a handkerchief around his head, looking like Aunt Jemima, going through his ritual. But it kept him going.

"Move Over, Gabriel." Louis' more than half a century of blowing and traveling finally took their toll. One day in the 1960s, while touring Italy, he collapsed. Joe Glaser happened to be ill in New York at the same time, and a wire that Pops sent him illustrates Louis' genial philosophy as well as his inimitable writing (and spelling) style: "You and I have no business dying. We were put here on earth for humanitarily purposes (Hmp). Did that come out of me? (Tee Hee). For the happiness of the people all over the world we must live longer than Mathusalem." Later on, in New York, he had to be hospitalized, but his spirits were high. "The doc says I've got very-close veins," he told me. "Nothin' that a little music won't cure." He then insisted that we rehearse a duet he wanted to use in the show.

Louis' last appearance, in March 1971, was at the Waldorf Astoria in New York. Although his once portly figure was wasted from illness, Pops was still there to "lay the music on the people." Doctors had warned him against blowing his trumpet, but he reached for those high notes just like old times.

After that he was hospitalized again and then had to rest at home. But every afternoon he would practice his trumpet. He sometimes spoke of death, but he had played too many of those wild New Orleans funerals to be maudlin. "I think I've had a beautiful life," he said. "I didn't wish for anything I couldn't get, and I got pretty near everything I wanted. They're going to enjoy blowing over me—cats will be coming from everywhere to play. Be good if I get to the Pearly Gates. I'll play a duet with Gabriel. Yeah. We'll play 'Sleepy Time Down South.'"

But Pops wasn't in any hurry for that duet. He was looking forward to going on the road again. "My chops is okay," he assured me. "All I need now is more strength in my treaders (legs)." Then, together, we played "Sleepy Time Down South." Several days later, on July 6, Louis died peacefully in his sleep.

His funeral was a simple one in a little church in the quiet neighborhood where he lived so long, but it was attended by many notables and televised by Telstar to 16 European nations. Peggy Lee sang the "Lord's Prayer" to the slow beat of a New Orleans funeral procession. Al Hibbler, the blind singer, sang "Nobody Knows the Trouble I've Seen." Disc jockey Freddie Robbins delivered a brief eulogy, concluding: "Move over, Gabriel, here comes Satchmo."

Then, as the funeral cortege rolled toward the cemetery, some kids held up a sign that read: "We all loved you, Louis." We all did.

The Wry Wit of Fred Allen

by James Harkins

Back in the days when vaudeville was going strong, I knew a young performer who used to write me marvelously witty letters as he shuttled around the country, hopping early-morning trains for one-night stands and split weeks. From Mason City, Iowa, he wrote: "These jumps will help me rise in show business. I had to rise at 3:45 to leave Cedar Rapids. I have to rise again at 6:45 to leave here for Clinton. Rip Van Winkle must have played a season out here, and took the 20-year rest to get acquainted with the mattress." From Centralia, Ill.: "This theater is so far back in the woods, the manager is a bear."

Many of you knew this man as Fred Allen, the star and principal writer of a long-running radio show that was a comedy classic. When I first met him he was Freddy James, 20 years old and living in a $4-a-week windowless room in a board-inghouse just off New York City's Broadway. "The halls were

43

so dark," he said, "the mice had a seeing-eye cat to lead them around."

In those days—1914—my wife and I were doing real good in vaudeville and Fred was having a rough time. He was *too* good, *too* bright for most audiences of the day, and a lot of theater managers canned him out of sheer bewilderment. Once he went onstage in a friend's act as the rear end of a horse, just to hear applause.

I'd say to him. "Freddy, you're too sophisticated. Take a few of my surefire gags." He'd grin and answer, "Naw, there must be some intelligent people around. I'll wait until I find them."

He billed himself originally as Freddy James, The World's Worst Juggler. Actually, he had been juggling—and not badly—since he was a kid. But when he learned he would never be a really great juggler, he decided to use his juggling just as a comic device. Ultimately he added a ventriloquist dummy (when he claimed to throw his voice, ushers in various parts of the theater would speak up) and a banjo to his act. He was very funny indeed, and gradually audiences began to appreciate him more.

Hoping to make the big time, he changed his name to Fred Allen (he had been born John Florence Sullivan, in Cambridge, Mass., in 1894). He made the change primarily so he wouldn't be confused with the Freddy James who had worked so cheap. To live up to his new name, he abandoned his old whiteface makeup, small derby, big shoes and comedy suit, and bought a tailor-made suit and snappy derby. He had, as he said, "so much class that I trespassed on the pretty."

On his first big-time two-a-day date in New York, however, he was fired before the evening show. Back in the small-time again, he added a sign to his act:

Mr. Allen Is Quite Deaf.
If You Care To
LAUGH OR APPLAUD
Please Do So
LOUDLY.

Finally, Jake and Lee Shubert signed him for *The Passing Show of 1922*, in which he wrote a lot of his own material and some for the stars, too. When the show went on the road, Allen had a good-sized part. One day the two railway cars in which the troupe was traveling were shifted by mistake to a siding and left there to bake under the hot sun—forever, apparently. Fred and another young comic, in pajamas, paraded through the cars, down the steps, and knelt in the hot cinders, praying:

> Now I lay me down to sleep.
> I pray the Lord my soul to keep.
> If I die before I wake,
> You tell Lee,
> I'll tell Jake.

Fred met Portland Hoffa, the prettiest chorus girl in *The Greenwich Village Follies*. They were married in 1927. Fred wrote a vaudeville act for the two of them—it was automatic for any true vaudevillian to put his wife immediately into his act—and they eventually played the mecca of vaudevillians, New York's Palace Theater.

Vaudeville, sadly, was on its last legs, shoved out by talking pictures. Fred's brand of sophisticated wit was catching on in New York, however. In the fall of 1932, when the new Broadway show he'd been promised failed to open, he wrote a radio show and sold it. Now he had found scope for his many talents. And Portland became a comedy star in her own right, thanks to a voice which sounded on radio, Fred used to say, like "two slate pencils mating."

I, on the other hand, was trying to support a wife and four children by putting on marathon dances in the hinterlands. Sundays, for an extra $35, I would take the train to New York from wherever I was and m.c. an amateur hour on station WMCA. One October Sunday in 1934, as I was leaving the radio station, I was told I was wanted on the telephone. Fred's wonderful, flat, nasal voice said: "Uncle Jim, how would you like to go to work for me?"

Five minutes later I was in Radio City, and we were shaking hands on a deal which lasted until Fred's death 22 years later. I ended by being a trouble shooter for him, taking care of all possible loose ends so he would be free from detail.

Those were the Depression days when "old friends" cut you dead on Broadway for fear you'd ask to borrow a buck. Fred, who'd been through bad times himself on the road, was the most open-handed man I have ever seen, and the quietest and most decent about it. Each morning he would fold 25 or 30 new dollar bills into squares not much bigger than postage stamps and drop them into his outside coat pocket. Then, on his way to work, he would hand out these little squares to the bums who were always waiting for him.

Once a pretty seedy-looking character stopped him on the street and said, "Mr. Allen, I hate to ask you, but $30 would save my life. I'm out of a job, and I'm being thrown out of my hotel because I owe that much room rent."

Fred looked him over carefully and said finally, "It wasn't Mr. Allen 35 years ago when we played the Gem in Peoria. In those days it was Freddy and Jack." He pulled a $100 bill from his wallet. Jack protested that he needed only $30. Fred said: "If I give you 30, you'll be just as bad off as before. Now what kind of job do you want?"

Jack said he was washed up in show business; what he wanted was some kind of job in the open air. Fred arranged through our current sponsor, Texaco, to get Jack work at a gas station in New Jersey. But Fred's interest didn't end there. Each week he made a point of telephoning the gas station to say, "This is Fred Allen. May I talk to my old friend Jack West, or is he too busy?"

Fred had two deep-seated prejudices: *organized* charities and vice presidents. He had a stubborn suspicion that the money paid into the big organized charities only paid for the fancy offices where the "molehill men" sat. A molehill man, according to Fred, was a "pseudo-busy executive who comes to work at 9 a.m. and finds a molehill on his desk. He has until 5 p.m. to make this molehill into a mountain. An accomplished molehill man will often have his mountain finished before lunch."

He demolished vice presidents with one memorable phrase: "The average vice president is a form of executive fungus which attaches itself to a desk."

In the early days of radio, there were a lot of vice presidents around—"treading bedlam," according to Fred, until some performer supplied a script. Then, just to have something to do, they cut it to ribbons. One night, after an encounter with what he considered some particularly stupid blue-penciling, he confided to the audience: "Come around some night before the show starts. At seven o'clock the vice presidents line up outside the door, and, at a given signal, go up-carpet to spawn."

The vice presidents, having rather underdeveloped bumps of humor, got their backs up and determined to cut Mr. Allen down to size. One vice president, whom I'll call Mr. X, was particularly determined—to his ultimate misfortune.

We did our "Allen's Alley" programs in NBC's big studio 8-H with a large audience. If the show was particularly good and the laughter went on longer than anticipated, we would have to struggle to finish on time. Sometimes we didn't make it. Whereupon Mr. X, instead of giving us an extra five seconds, would chop Fred off in the middle of a word. This annoyed Fred; so, as a "public service" one week he started his next show with the end of his previous program, to give the listener an idea of what they had missed the preceding week.

One day Fred received word that Mr. X had blue-penciled one whole page out of his script, and that if Fred used that page he would be cut off the air. Fred used the page—and was off the air for one minute and ten seconds in the middle of the show.

The NBC switchboard was choked with calls asking what was wrong. Newspapers began to call up. Mr. X at first insisted that there had been "mechanical difficulties." When word seeped out as to what had really happened, he finally said he had shut Allen off the air because of "objectionable material." So I leaked this "objectionable material" to the press. Part of it went this way:

PORTLAND: Why were you cut off last Sunday?

ALLEN: Who knows? The main thing in radio is to come out on time. If people laugh, the program is longer. The thing to do is to get a nice dull half hour. Nobody will laugh or applaud. Then you'll always be right on time, and all of the little emaciated radio executives can dance around their desks in interoffice abandon.

PORTLAND: Radio sure is funny.

ALLEN: All except the comedy programs. Our program has been cut off so many times the last page of the script is a Band-Aid.

At a stockholders' meeting a few days later, the president

of NBC was asked about the incident. His answer was short and to the point: "It was a mistake. The person who made it is no longer with us."

Fred didn't gloat, nor did he rest on his laurels. He wrote a modest letter to the thousands of people who had written him and added this prickly postscript: "All NBC vice presidents have been ordered to acquire a sense of humor immediately. Until each vice president can learn to laugh, a hyena is being placed in his office to react audibly to anything funny that may come up."

I think Fred Allen was the greatest humorist since Mark Twain. His wit was especially effective in dealing with awkward or exasperating situations. One day in Radio City a big jerk grabbed Fred's arm and, in an intimate gesture which made Fred cringe, picked a piece of imaginary lint off his lapel. Fred said icily, "Put that back!"

When he was in Hollywood, Fred wrote us: "All the sincerity out here you could stuff in a flea's navel and still have room to conceal eight caraway seeds and an agent's heart." When Hedda Hopper asked him to stay there over Christmas for a big party, he told her: "Hedda, at Christmas, the wise men went East."

We had a conference room at NBC with nothing printed on the door. As a result, our sessions were invariably punctuated by a succession of people Fred used to call "peepers," who would open the door, look in and leave without a word. One day the telephone rang, but nobody was at the other end. Fred commented: "Probably one of the peepers who couldn't make it today."

In June 1949 Fred went off the air. His health—he had very high blood pressure and was on a salt-free diet for years—prevented him from making what I am sure would have been a unique imprint on television. But it didn't prevent him from poking fun at TV. He figured out an idea for a television quiz show. The panel would consist of doctors, the contestants would wear hospital gowns, and the title of the program would be: "What's My Disease?"

Fred lived for his work, for the friends he made through it, and for Portland. He and Portland were together constantly. She would cook dinner for the two of them, and Fred would wash the dishes afterward while she dried. Later, while he worked, she would sit and knit, not saying a word. When he was through for the night, the two of them would go for a walk—sometimes 20 or 30 blocks—until he was ready for sleep. Fred dedicated his book, *Treadmill to Oblivion*: "To Portland, who stayed in a closet until I finished writing this book."

On March 17, 1956, he was close to finishing a second book. Around 3 a.m. he put aside his work and asked Portland if she wanted to take a walk with him. It was cold and windy, and she begged off. He dropped dead just around the corner from their apartment.

I can still feel him walking down the street beside me, making those wonderful wry cracks in that nasal voice. Once he pointed at some rolls of telephone cable and said, "Dental floss for Martha Raye, Jim." I feel like the luckiest guy in the world because I had the privilege of knowing Fred Allen and Freddy James—and loving both of them.

Life is a Banquet

*by Rosalind Russell, Chris Chase and
Frederick Brisson*

*Producer Freddie Brisson and actress Rosalind Russell were
an unusual couple in Hollywood annals. They worked together,
they loved and respected each other—and they were married
for 35 years. Through a best-selling autobiography, with a
foreword by her husband, we are witness to an amazing
woman's warmth, vitality and unforgettable courage. In these
excerpts from both foreword and book, Freddie Brisson speaks
first.*

In this autobiography, Rosalind has devoted a few paragraphs
to the cancer that eventually killed her. Asked why she hadn't
written more, she said, "One disease to a book is enough."

After she died, I found a petition she had tucked away in
her prayer book. It said in part, "Keep my mind free from the
recital of endless details; give me wings to get to the point.
Seal my lips on aches and pains."

She never wanted to bore an audience; she never wanted anybody else to bore an audience on her behalf. Being a proud and doting husband, I once added to her professional credits for the press a list of 115 awards and citations—and 94 civic and public-spirited activities in which she'd been involved.

She hated it. "Will you quit handing out that thing to people, Freddie? It's embarrassing."

We decided on the book's title—*Life Is A Banquet*—not simply because she created the character of "Auntie Mame," but because one of Mame's lines summed up Rosalind's philosophy: "Live, live, live," Mame would admonish. "Life is a banquet, and most of you suckers are starving to death!"

That aliveness of Rosalind's bowled me over when I first saw her on the screen in "The Women," in 1939. That's for me, I thought. I was newly arrived from England, staying with my old friend Cary Grant, who was filming "His Girl Friday" with Rosalind. Cary assured me that it would be easy to bring us together. He invited her for Christmas. She sent regrets. He invited her for our New Year's Eve party. She never showed.

Finally it happened. Rosalind tells how.

Toward the end of "His Girl Friday," Cary started talking about Freddie Brisson. "You know Freddie Brisson?" he'd ask. And I'd say, "No, what is that, a sandwich?" And he'd say, "No, this guy, Freddie Brisson."

When this roundabout approach failed, Cary took more direct action. One night we had a date to go dancing and, when I went to the door to let him in, Cary was standing there with another man. Cary looked sheepish. "This," he said, "is Freddie Brisson."

After that evening Freddie phoned me every day for nine months straight. Finally, I felt sorry for him and let him take me to the races. Then we went on a boat trip to Catalina.

Still, I didn't take Freddie seriously until the night Broadway critic John McClain called and asked me to a party for British War Relief. I said, "No, John, I can't go. I'm going with Freddie Brisson." And as I hung up I thought, that's very intersting. Why did I do that?

The first time I proposed, she didn't accept. But I persisted. "There's no way I'm going to get rid of you, is there?" Rosalind finally said, laughing. But when she gave in, it was on her own terms. "I don't like these proposals after you've had an evening out. If you want to propose, then come around at seven o'clock in the morning and put a white handkerchief on the ground and kneel down and ask for my hand."

At seven o'clock the next morning Roz accepted. (They were married on October 25, 1941.)

In the 35 years we were married we never gave each other ultimatums: Neither of us ever said, "If that's the way you feel about it, I'm going to the Beverly Hills Hotel." Roz believed you should never go to bed angry. If she was very mad at me, and locked her door, I'd phone her: "I'm trying to live by *your* rule. Unlock the door so I can come in and kiss you." She'd unlock the door, still looking a little angry, and we would hug each other and say good-night.

Financially, Roz gave up a good deal for our marriage. Metro-Goldwyn-Mayer had offered her the same kind of contract Clark Gable had—$7500 a week, 52 weeks a year—and she said no. "If I sign that, my life will belong to Metro and not to us."

It has been said that if a performer is lucky, he gets one great hit—maybe two—in his life. For me it was certainly "Auntie Mame," which opened on Broadway in 1956.

People loved the character. When I walked about the streets of New York, truckdrivers leaned out of their windows and yelled, "Hello, Mame!"

Even the great English actress Dame Sybil Thorndike was said to "adore" Mame, and one evening I went to an after-theater supper to meet her. When I arrived, she was sitting down, looking like a queen on a throne. Allowing me to take her hand, Dame Sybil went on about what a superb actress I was, how I'd given one of the great performances of the season; as a matter of fact, of all time. She ended by saying, "You are absolutely fabulous in 'Orpheus Descending.' "

She had the wrong actress. Keeps you humble.

Later on, when "Mame" was turned into a musical, I was asked to play the part. I said no, I've done it.

Turn the page, move on.

Roz was a fighter. She never complained. In 1960, after her first mastectomy, she went to fashion designer Galanos. She came into his office very businesslike. "I'm going to tell you something nobody else in the world knows except Freddie and my doctor. I've had a breast removed and I want to keep it quiet." (Women had not yet begun to tell about their breast cancers.)

Then she started to cry, and Galanos saw that she could hardly lift her left arm, it was so swollen, and he broke down too. From that day forward he designed all her clothing, and he never told a soul.

I'll brag about Freddie. Why he doesn't get discouraged, I'll never know. A producer has to fight every inch of the way, straighten out every writer, go over every costume, every set, fight with everybody. I'm talking about real working producers, not the ones who are called in at the last moment with money.

Often I wonder how I lucked into this guy. Whenever we were home together in the old days, we danced in the hall after dinner. We'd get right up from the table, put on Guy Lombardo records, and we'd twirl. I'd be saying, "Bend me back, don't drop me," and Freddie would be saying, "Ah, the sweetest music this side of heaven."

Freddie was reared a Catholic, and he has a very deep faith, unadorned, direct. He's a good person, and I've never known him to hurt anyone. I worry about him, and I wish I knew how to keep him from overworking.

Lucky is the word I come back to. I got lucky.

In 1965 Roz had a second mastectomy. In 1969 she was hit by severe rheumatoid arthritis, and in April 1975 by pneumonia. Then in the fall of 1975, the cancer recurred.

In 1976, after she'd undergone a hip operation, I brought her home from the hospital for the last time. It was October 5, three weeks before our 35th anniversary, and she was already worrying about what to get me. She had a new sports jacket in mind and threatened to burn the old one I had worn to the hospital.

The morning of our anniversary I fixed her breakfast tray with a little bouquet of bouvardia, an exotic white flower I had worn and Roz had carried on our wedding day. Beside it I put a letter in which I'd tried to say all the things you can never really say.

That night she came downstairs to dinner. She'd been staying up in her bedroom, but now, as a gesture for our son Lance, his wife and me, she dressed in her best hostess gown.

I'd ordered a dinner I though she might enjoy, we drank a glass of champagne and there was a wedding cake. I gave her a tiny bracelet made of very thin gold, with the number 35 spelled out in diamond baguettes, and when Roz opened the box and saw it, her eyes shone. She looked like she was 12 years old. "I'll never take it off," she said. And she never did.

She died on November 28. My life goes on. The days are easier than the nights. I have a hard time sleeping.

But Rosalind would not want to be remembered in sadness. In this book, she recalls the lines of Greek poet Pindar who, 500 years before Christ, wrote: "We are things of a day.... The shadow of a dream is man, no more. But when the brightness comes, and God gives it, there is a shining of light on men and their life is sweet."

My life has been sweet. If I could wave a magic wand and alter the past, I'd only relax my tendency to push too hard. It's always mañana time for me. Next month I'll take it easy. Freddie and I will go to Hawaii and have a fine rest together, and that will be lovely. But it doesn't happen.

I think the older you get, the more you are struck by that brightness God gives, the more you find light alone to be a wonderful thing, the more you feel there's something else.

Elvis, the Man

by Jon Bradshaw

He was called the King. Also Elvis the Pelvis, Swivel Hips, the Hillbilly Cat and Mamma Presley's Son.

He lived in Memphis, on Elvis Presley Boulevard. His eyes were blue. He was six feet tall and weighed 230 pounds. His hair was light brown but was dyed black and sprayed with lacquer. In his heyday, he earned between $5 million and $6 million a year.

He was born shortly after noon on January 8, 1935, in a two-room shack in Tupelo, Miss. His father worked crops and delivered milk; his mother was a sewing-machine operator. His twin brother, Jesse Garon, was born dead.

He was taught to say "ma'am" and "sir" and to stand when his elders entered the room. At the age of ten, he won second prize in a local talent contest by standing on a chair and singing "Old Shep" unaccompanied. His mother saved for five months and bought Elvis his first guitar. It cost $12.95.

In 1948, his parents moved to Memphis in order to begin a new life. The combined Presley family income was now $35 a week. Elvis's eighth-grade music teacher claimed that the youngster showed very little promise.

He graduated from Humes High School in Memphis in 1953. That summer he worked as a truck driver, earning $41 a week, while at night he studied to become an electrician.

His first professional record, "That's All Right, Mama," with "Blue Moon of Kentucky" on the flip side, was released in August 1954 on the Sun label. When the record was first aired on the radio, Elvis hid in a Memphis theater, afraid that his friends would laugh at him. The record was not a success. A Memphis disc jockey said that Elvis was so "country" he should not be played after 5 a.m.

Even so, Elvis, his guitarist and his bass player, a group billed as the Blue Moon Boys, began touring the rural South and Southwest. While on the road, Elvis couldn't sleep at night unless he phoned his mother first. He began including his famous wiggle in the act. His fans would become hysterical. "I don't even know I'm doing it," said Elvis. "But the more I do it, the wilder they get."

He appeared at Nashville's Grand Ole Opry. Jim Denny, who headed the Opry's talent office, told Elvis afterward that he should consider driving a truck again. Elvis cried all the way back to Memphis. But at a concert in Florida, teen-agers savaged his pink jacket and ripped off his white shoes.

In late 1955, tough Col. Tom Parker became Presley's manager and negotiated a deal with Sun Records in which RCA bought Presley's contract for $35,000. Elvis's first record for RCA was "Heartbreak Hotel." It zoomed to No. 1 and remained there for eight weeks.

Nineteen fifty-six was Elvis Presley's year. "Heartbreak Hotel," "Hound Dog," "Don't Be Cruel" and "Love Me Tender" were all No. 1 hits. Ed Sullivan, who had said that Elvis was unfit for family viewing, put him on his television show, and some 54 million viewers watched (although "The Pelvis" was shown only from the waist up).

The act caused a public outcry. Elvis was hanged in effigy in Nashville and burned in absentia in St. Louis. Billy Graham said he wouldn't want *his* children to witness Presley. Florida banned the Presley bump and grind. "They all think I'm a sex maniac," said Elvis. "But I'm just being natural."

By the end of 1956, there were some 78 separate Elvis Presley products on the market, from Elvis Presley bubble-gum cards to Elvis Presley Bermuda shorts to Elvis Presley photographs that glowed in the dark. It is estimated that he grossed $100 million in his first two years of stardom.

He had three jet airplanes, two Cadillacs, a Rolls-Royce, a Lincoln Continental, Buick and Chrysler station wagons, a Jeep, a dune buggy, a converted bus and three motorcycles—and a habit of giving Cadillacs and Continentals to his friends.

Perhaps his favorite car was his 1960 Cadillac 75 limousine. The top was covered with pearl-white Naugahyde, and the body was sprayed with 40 coats of a special paint that included crushed diamonds and fish scales. Nearly all the metal trim was plated with 18-karat gold. There were gold records in the ceiling. The rear windows were covered with gold-lamé draperies. There were two gold-flake telephones. There was a gold vanity case, containing a gold electric razor and gold hair clippers, an electric shoe buffer, a gold-plated television set, a phonograph, a multiplex amplifier, air conditioning, an electrical system for operating any household appliance and a refrigerator that made ice in precisely two minutes.

By late 1956, Elvis was too popular to go out into the streets. He took to renting skating rinks, amusement parks or cinemas for the entire night, and he and his friends skated, rode the Dodg'em cars or watched film after film till dawn.

On March 24, 1958, he was inducted into the Army. Physically, he was sound; mentally, average. While in the Army, Elvis took a cut in pay—from over $100,000 a month to $78. He drove a Jeep, learned karate and was promoted to sergeant. And he often received 10,000 letters a week.

On May 1, 1967, he married Priscilla Beaulieu, a 21-year-old girl he had met while in the Army. Nine months to the day of the marriage, Priscilla gave birth to Presley's only child, a daughter named Lisa Marie.

Throughout the '60s, Elvis was the most highly paid entertainer in the world. In 1960, he received the highest fee ever paid for a single guest appearance on television until that time— $125,000 for a Frank Sinatra special. He sold more then 500 million records, and made 33 films. (*King Creole* was his favorite; he hated most of the rest.) And between 1957 and

1967, he gave away more than $1 million to charities, acquaintances and friends.

Elvis made no public appearances between 1961 and 1968. He had no No. 1 hit songs between the spring of 1962 and the autumn of 1969. In 1973, he and his wife were divorced.

He worried constantly about his weight. While watching himself in his old movies, he occasionally slumped in his seat, muttering, "No, no, too fat, too fat." But he loved such foods as peanut butter and mashed-banana sandwiches, banana splits, olives and burnt bacon. He suffered from hypertension, an impacted or enlarged colon, mild diabetes and a liver problem.

Elvis had a violent temper and was known to smash up television sets and pool tables. He also collected Teddy bears, and rarely drank anything but Mountain Valley spring water, Gatorade, Pepsi, and Nesbitt's orange soda.

When making public appearances, he wore a bulletproof vest. When he rented a Memphis cinema at night, guests of his friends were frisked before the film began. And he was always surrounded by an entourage of as many as 12 men. They were known as the Memphis Mafia.

Once, when Elvis had a cold, one of his entourage found him in his music room playing "How Great Thou Art" on the piano. "How do you feel?" the minion asked.

"Alone," said the King.

...And The Elvis Mystique

by Alice Anne Conner

For me, New Year's Eve will always be filled with images and impressions of the first man I was ever (maybe ever will be) in love with—old Swivel Hips himself.

It goes back to when I was 12 and my parents took me with them to the "Louisiana Hayride" show in Shreveport. They had decided to attend this particular Hayride for three reasons: It was my cousin Maurice's birthday and, since we were staying at his mother's house, we had to do *something* special for him; and because my dad and mother loved country music (especially the featured star, Ferlin Husky). And because there wasn't much else to do in Shreveport on New Year's Eve, 1955.

Now Ferlin Husky, you may recall, was a pretty popular country-and-western singer back in '55. He made my mother's eyes light up and my father's feet start tapping.(*I* thought his hair looked greasy.)

Ferlin had just finished his act—and I my hot dog—when it happened. From the wings of the stage someone called the "Hillbilly Cat" sped out like a whirling bullet in an orange suit, white cowboy hat and black boots. He was the most beautiful thing I'd ever seen. There I sat, 12 years old and never kissed, watching my fantasies singing and dancing right in front of my eyes.

Elvis did his rendition of "Heartbreak Hotel," and I wept. When he told me not to step on his "Blue Suede Shoes," I would have killed anyone who dared try. He sang "Peace in the Valley," and I wanted to sing praises to the Lord.

Lest you think I was particularly sophomoric, let me tell you about the rest of the audience.

My father said, "Damn, that boy's got something!"

My mother wasn't quite as reserved: "Now *that* boy can eat crackers in my bed anytime!"

All around us, people—children, teen-agers, adults and senior citizens—were clapping, singing, standing, jumping and having a grand ole time. Then, just as suddenly as it had begun, it was over, and Elvis had twirled off the stage as dynamically as he'd twirled on.

The announcer told all of us we could get pictures of our favorite Hayride stars outside in the lobby for just one dollar, and if we hurried we could get them autographed personally right down the way by the Coca-Cola stand.

My father reached into his pocket. "Here, baby," he said to me. "Go downstairs there and get us a picture of Ferlin Husky and go on and get him to sign it for us. That thing'll be worth something someday, I betcha."

Well, I guess it's hard for anyone to understand how a person could get Ferlin Husky and Elvis Presley mixed up. But heaven help me, I did.

I approached the counter: "I'd like a picture of Ferlin Huskey, please." With Ferlin in hand, I walked toward the Coca-Cola stand.

Then I saw the orange suit.

I got in line, my mind and body absolutely reeling with the excitement of it all. I couldn't believe I was only 15 people away, 14, 13, 12. . . .

"Hi, honey. You shore do look pretty tonight. Want me to sign this?"

I nodded, thunderstruck.

He looked at the picture, then turned those incredible blue eyes toward me.

"You want me to sign *this* picture, honey?"

I nodded again.

"Well, babe, if it'll make you happy."

Somehow, I found my way back upstairs, collapsed into my chair and handed the 8-by-10 glossy to my mother.

"Look what she did!" she said to my father. "Look what she did! Why'd she do that?" (My mother never has understood me.)

"Well, I'll be," my father said, irritated more than just a bit. "You think dollar bills grow on trees? Now what've we got? A picture of Ferlin Husky signed by that damn boy!"

After things settled down, we took cousin Maurice and Aunt Beulah to this sleazy little Chinese restaurant. As I sat staring at the plastic-flower decorations that were set beside the Tabasco bottle, the door opened. I thought I had died and gone to heaven.

There he was! Elvis Presley in the flesh! He had changed from the orange suit to a blue shirt, black cowboy sports coat, and black pants—pegged at the ankle.

My stomach flopped over, and I spilled my Coke. Elvis looked at me, curled his lip, threw a kiss, then winked.

I should have died right then, because I had never been before, nor have I ever been since, as happy as I was at that moment.

He winked at me!

A few months later, we were sitting at my grandmother's house watching "The Steve Allen Show."

"And here, ladies and gentlemen, direct from the 'Louisiana Hayride' with his big hit, 'Heartbreak Hotel,' is the up-and-coming singing sensation—*Elvis Presley!*"

We watched, mesmerized. No longer was he the Hillbilly Cat. He was ELVIS!

"Would you look at that," my father said.

"We saw him, didn't we?" my mother said.

"Cheap," my grandfather said, noting the glint in my eyes.

"He's right pretty," my grandmother said, understanding the glint.

Several times in the next few years my father asked me what in the world ever happened to that Ferlin Husky picture that Elvis Presley autographed.

I'd say, "I don't know. Must have been lost in one of our moves."

"Well," Daddy would say, "it don't matter much, 'cause he probably won't last."

And I would close my eyes and smile, remembering that orange suit and Elvis saying "honey" and throwing me that kiss. And let me tell you something, folks. *That* lasts.

A Streak of Violence

Secrets of a Soviet Assassin

by Isaac Don Levine

"I put my raincoat on the table so that I could take out the *piolet* [ice ax] in the pocket. When Trotsky started to read my article, I took the ax and, closing my eyes, gave him a tremendous blow on the head.

"The man screamed in a way that I will never forget— *Aaaa!* . . . very long, infinitely long. He got up like a madman, threw himself at me and bit my hand—look, you can still see the marks of his teeth. Then I pushed him, so he fell to the floor."

With these words the most celebrated and mysterious assassin of our time—the man who called himself Jacques Mornard—described his murder of Leon Trotsky, exiled patriarch of Bolshevism. It took place on August 20, 1940, inside the steel-shuttered walls of Trotsky's heavily guarded villa on the outskirts of Mexico City. "Mornard" was convicted and sentenced to 20 years' imprisonment in the Mexican Federal Penitentiary.

For all that time he resolutely refused to disclose his identity, motives or political ties. Despite the mask, his true identity was gradually pieced together over the years. He was Ramon Mercader del Rio, a Spaniard, Moscow-trained in the art of murder. He killed Trotsky on the orders of the world's most fearsome secret-police organization, the Soviet State Security, then called the NKVD. But his stubborn refusal to admit his identity enabled the organizers of the crime to disavow any connection with it.

When he was arrested, the police found on him a three-page statement, typewritten in French, dated and signed at the last moment in pencil. It stated that he was the son of "an old Belgian family," that he had been caught up in the Trotskyite movement while studying journalism in Paris. He had met Trotsky and become disenchanted, the "confession" said, and finally moved to kill him when the old Bolshevik tried to force him to go to the Soviet Union to organize an assassination plot against Stalin.

These claims, and amplifying details the prisoner gave after his arrest, were quickly proved absurd: the people, schools and addresses he mentioned were nonexistent or totally unlike his descriptions. But no logic could make him change his story.

For six months "Mornard" was given an intensive psychological examination by Dr. José Gomez Robleda, head of the department of medical-biological studies at the National University of Mexico, and Dr. Alfonso Quiroz Cuaron, professor of criminology. At first suspicious of the doctors, the prisoner gradually came to talk freely with them. Though he never disclosed anything he considered important, he unwittingly revealed a great deal about himself.

The two doctors found the killer a truly extraordinary man. He was fluent in several languages. Attractive to women, he could be ingratiating to men, and would pass for a gentleman anywhere. He had superior intelligence, remarkable self-possession, a gift for acting. He displayed a marked interest in gambling, mountain climbing, small-craft sailing. His coordination, dexterity and mechanical aptitudes were unusual: given a Mauser rifle, he proceeded to dismantle it in the dark and put it back together in less than four minutes.

His responses to word-association tests showed the prisoner to be deeply indoctrinated in Stalinist views, and he betrayed his Moscow training on several occasions. At one point, for example, he made a passing reference to a man named Kamo—a figure almost unknown in the West but a hero within the NKVD, whose history was taught in Soviet schools for infiltration and sabotage. A test of "Mornard's" pronunciation showed that his "native French," although excellent, bore traces of a Spanish accent, and he showed a striking familiarity with anything Spanish. The evidence suggested a Spanish Communist background.

But it was not until September 1950 that Dr. Quiroz Cuaron was able to document the suspicions. The criminologist found his proof in police archives in Madrid: the dusty fingerprints of a man named Ramon Mercader, arrested in Barcelona in 1935 as a Communist youth organizer, tallied with those of "Mornard." So did pictures.

Don Pablo Mercader Marina, a tall elderly man living in retirement in Barcelona, took a good look at a photograph of the Trotsky killer. "Yes," he said, "that's my son." Don Pablo did not know of his son's crime. Long removed from the family, he said, "I do not want to reestablish contact with any of them."

Further revelations by ex-Communists established additional facts in Mornard-Mercader's strange history. This is the story:

Ramon Mercader was born in Barcelona in 1913, the second child of Caridad del Rio Hernandez and Don Pablo, a conservative gentleman of good but not too prosperous family. Ramon's mother, a spirited young society matron, was a strikingly attractive woman, quick-tempered and unpredictable, who at the dangerous age of 33 developed a compulsion to adventure. She began to associate with Bohemians and revolutionaries, and in 1925 she moved to France. Here she joined the Communist Party, had numerous love affairs with French Communist leaders, and worked as an underground courier.

Ramon, who lived part of the time with his mother, part with his father, worshiped his mother and was soon drawn into her Communist associations. When the Spanish Civil War started in 1936, he and his mother were among the first to volunteer to fight Franco.

At this point a new love entered the life of Caridad Mercader: Leonid Eitingon, a general in the NKVD who, under the name of General Kotov, was organizing Loyalist commando and sabotage units in Spain. One of his students was Ramon Mercader. What neither Ramon nor Caridad may have known at this time was that Eitingon was also a leading officer of a special NKVD division in charge of liquidating Soviet political enemies on foreign soil. Their No. 1 target was Leon Trotsky.

Lev Davidovich Bronstein, known to the world as Leon Trotsky, had designed and engineered with Lenin the Bolshevik Revolution of November 1917. Stalin was at the time a semiobscure henchman of Lenin's, but after Lenin's death he maneuvered to isolate Trotsky politically, and in 1929 he expelled him from the Soviet Union. Since then Trotsky had lived the life of a hunted man, pursued by Stalin's killers from one place to another. One by one his retinue was picked off: his secretary was killed in Spain; his son died suddenly in Paris, and Trotskyites believed he had been poisoned. Finally, in 1937, Trotsky sought refuge in Mexico.

Caridad and Ramon were now in Moscow with Eitingon, and Ramon was receiving highly specialized training in the arts of terror. Plans for the great assassination were already being laid. What kind of a man was needed to deal with Trotsky in Mexico? Spanish-speaking Ramon Mercader must have seemed an obvious choice.

In the Byzantine way of the Soviet secret police, it was decided that Mercader should ingratiate himself with the Trotsky household by seducing one of its female couriers, Sylvia Ageloff, a young American social worker and loyal member of the U.S. Trotskyite group. The NKVD arranged for Ramon to meet Sylvia "by chance" in Paris in the summer of 1938. Young, personable, well-supplied with money, he must have looked like the answer to a young woman's prayer. He became her constant companion.

Ramon followed Sylvia to New York on a false passport issued in the name of "Frank Jacson." (The original from which this passport was drawn had been taken from a Canadian who was killed in Spain with the International Brigade. Embarrassingly, Soviet technical documentation experts had misspelled the name: it should have been "Jackson.") Sylvia and he took a temporary apartment in Greenwich Village. Then "Jacson" announced that he had been offered a job in Mexico

City, and in January 1940 Sylvia followed him there. Eitingon was in Mexico to supervise the assassination, and with him was Caridad Mercader.

Ramon's role at this point, Caridad had assured a friend, was solely that of a spy—to find out the nature of the security system at Trotsky's villa at Coyoacán, a Mexico City suburb. Through Sylvia he gained entree. During visits there, although he did not at first meet Trotsky, Ramon roamed through the house, snapping pictures with a concealed camera but relying on his photographic memory for most of the details. His material was sent to Moscow and placed in a special dossier of the NKVD. (Vladimir Petrov, the Soviet intelligence officer who defected in Australia in April 1954, saw this dossier in 1948. It contained "complete documentation of Trotsky's life right up to his last days.")

In the early morning hours of May 24, 1940, the Soviet spy command in Mexico tried an audacious frontal assault on the Trotsky dwelling. A group of 20 men, dressed in Mexican police and army uniforms, drove up to the residence, stormed through the gate, and delivered murderous submachine-gun fire into the bedrooms where the Trotskys and their 11-year-old grandson were sleeping.

Amazingly, Trotsky, his wife and grandchild survived the attack—by throwing themselves under their beds. After a month's investigation, the Mexican police cracked the case, and some two dozen persons were arrested and later tried. Ramon Mercader, however, remained above suspicion.

Only four days after the armed attack, Mercader offered to drive Mrs. Trotsky to Vera Cruz with some mutual friends. It was on this occasion that Ramon first met his future victim. He entered the villa's courtyard and chatted briefly and courteously with Trotsky. He gave Trotsky's grandson a small glider as a present. Only a man of iron nerve could have carried on with such an assignment so soon after an attempted assassination which he had helped to stage.

Moscow now decided on a single-handed assassination attempt, and Ramon was to play the lead. Caridad arranged with the NKVD for maximum safeguards and a chance for her son to escape alive.

Mercader—or "Jacson," as he was known to most of the Trotskyites—stepped up the pace of his infiltration program.

During the last three weeks in July he paid the Trotskys five visits, never neglecting such friendly little gestures as bringing candy for Mrs. Trotsky.

On August 17 Ramon visited the master with the outline of an article he was writing. Trotsky had agreed to check it over. The two men spent 11 minutes alone in Trotsky's study. Trotsky remarked to his wife afterward that the young man's behavior had seemed strange. That visit was the "dress rehearsal."

On August 20 Sylvia and Ramon ran into one of the Trotsky bodyguards downtown. The "Jacsons" said they were returning to the United States the next day, but would say good-by to Trotsky first. Ramon excused himself and departed on some urgent business. Sylvia went back to their hotel and awaited a message from him. He never returned.

At 5:20 that afternoon Ramon Mercader showed up at the Trotsky villa with his completed article to show Trotsky. He was carrying a khaki raincoat. Sewn into it was a long dagger, and in one pocket he carried the ice ax, its stock cut down for easy concealment. In the back pocket of his trousers he carried a .45-caliber automatic. He hoped to accomplish his murderous mission with a single crushing blow of the ice ax, which would make little noise and thus enable him to get away quietly and unmolested. If any mishap should occur, he had the automatic to shoot his way out.

The guards recognized him and opened the double electric doors of the fortress villa without hesitation. One guard led him to Trotsky, who was feeding his pet rabbits in the courtyard. Mrs. Trotsky saw him, noticed his raincoat and commented that it was somewhat incongruous on such a sunny day. "Yes, but you know it won't last long—it might rain," Ramon said, holding the bulky coat close to his body.

Trotsky obviously did not want to tear himself away from the rabbits, but finally he took off his working gloves and walked into the house. Ramon followed him to the study, where Trotsky closed the door and sat down at his worktable. A few inches from his hand was a loaded .25-caliber automatic. Ramon stood at his left side, blocking off the switch to the house alarm system.

Trotsky took the article and started to read. At that exact moment Ramon seized the ice ax and, closing his eyes, smashed it down on his victim's skull, penetrating almost three inches into the brain.

With a fearful cry, Trotsky threw himself at the killer and grappled with him. Mrs. Trotsky rushed to the study to find her husband stumbling dazedly from the room. "See what they have done to me!" he said, and slumped to the floor.

Trotsky's bodyguards swarmed into the room now. Ramon stood gasping, face knotted, pistol dangling in his hand. The bodyguards began to hammer away at him. Mrs. Trotsky addressed a curiously detached question to her still conscious husband. "What about that one?" she asked, gesturing toward the assassin. "They will kill him."

"No . . . impermissible to kill," Trotsky said slowly. "He must be forced to talk." Rushed to the hospital, Trotsky soon lapsed into unconsciousness. He was operated on, but he died 26 hours later.

A block away Caridad was sitting in a chauffeur-driven car, a bizarre parody of the anxious mother waiting for her son to come home from work. General Eitingon was waiting in another car nearby. When the police alarm sounded and an ambulance came through the streets, they realized that Ramon had not got away. Caridad drove immediately to the airport and, with a forged passport, made her way to Cuba. Eitingon drove all night to Acapulco, where he boarded a Soviet freighter waiting in the harbor.

Some weeks later Caridad rejoined Eitingon in Moscow. There Lavrenti Beria, head of the NKVD, himself presented her to Stalin. She received the Order of Lenin—Communism's highest decoration—and her son was cited as a Hero of the Soviet Union. To a friend in Moscow she proudly spoke of these honors.

Caridad spent the war years in the Soviet Union, receiving assurances from her lover Eitingon and his Kremlin superiors that an operation to rescue her son would be launched. Stalin proved reluctant to redeem the pledge, but eventually allowed her to try to organize an escape. She arrived in Mexico City in March 1945, but was unable to achieve her objective—or even to see her son, so ironclad was the regime imposed on her by the NKVD to ensure the secrecy of the assassin's identity.

Subsequently, Caridad lived in Paris amid disillusionment.

The years in the Soviet Union served to cure her of some of her Communism. "You are right," she said in Moscow to an intimate Spanish comrade of independent views. "We have been deceived. This is not paradise. It is hell."

Sylvia Ageloff, when she learned that her lover had killed Trotsky, went into a nervous collapse from which it took years to recover. (Ramon wept when he was told of this in prison, but later he lost all interest in her.) She finally married and lived quietly in New York City. Trotsky's widow remained for years in the same house in Coyoacán. Eitingon died a victim—with his master, Beria—of the 1953 purges after Stalin's death.

Mercader became Mexico's model prisoner. He ran the penitentiary radio-repair shop, a small but profitable business. He was comfortable, having taken advantage of the lenient Mexican prison regulations to ensure special food, books and other comforts. Double-chinned and corpulent, he began to look like a relaxed bourgeois businessman. He had few friends inside prison, but operated his radio shop with cool efficiency, read fitfully—and through underground channels kept in touch with the Communist network outside.

He never stopped giving his name as Jacques Mornard.

Upon release from prison in 1960, Mercader went to Cuba. Fifteen days later he flew to Prague, then to Moscow, where he lived until his death in 1979.

Mike Malloy vs. The Murder Trust

by Irving Wallace

Michael Malloy was surely the most durable human in American history. Over 30 attempts were made to murder him. He survived all but the last.

The 60-year-old Malloy was a bleary-eyed, unsteady little Irishman originally from County Donegal. In better times he had been a fireman; now, in the dreary Depression winter of 1933, his full-time occupation was alcoholic, and his favorite speak-easy was Tony Marino's place on Third Avenue in New York City's Bronx.

It was at Marino's that he first came to the attention of The Murder Trust. Actually, members of The Trust (so named later by tabloid newspapers) were less impressive than that grand title implied. They were a mixed lot with just two things in common—they all hung out at Marino's, and they all needed money.

The mainstays of The Trust were: Anthony Marino, 27,

proprietor of the speakeasy; Joseph Murphy, 28, a onetime chemist, now bartender; Francis Pasqua, 24, an undertaker; and Daniel Kreisberg, 29, a fruit vendor. On a cold January night the quartet gathered at Marino's to discuss their bleak financial status. Spotting Michael Malloy trying to wheedle a drink, Pasqua had an idea: "Why don't we take out insurance on Malloy, like Tony did with Betty Carlson?"

He was referring to the spring of 1932, when, desperate for cash, Marino had taken out a $2000 insurance policy on his girlfriend, a young blonde named Betty Carlson. Then, on a particularly cold night, Miss Carlson, insensible from alcohol, had been stripped, laid out on her bed and doused with cold water. The windows of her room were thrown open, and in the morning she was dead of pneumonia and alcoholism. And the insurance company paid off.

Pasqua's idea met with favor, and eventually not one policy but three were taken out on Malloy, who was identified as a relative of bartender Joseph Murphy. One $800 policy was obtained from Metropolitan Life; two $494 policies were obtained from Prudential. A double-indemnity clause was included. The $1788 of insurance would be worth $3576 if Malloy should die by accident.

The first day that the policies were safely in pocket, the killing of Michael Malloy got under way. When he weaved into Marino's that afternoon, the proprietor greeted him warmly and announced that, because of competition, he was relaxing his credit restrictions. Malloy's watery eyes shone, and he began to down shots of whiskey nonstop.

Initially, Marino and company had theorized that Malloy was so debilitated by years of drinking that an excessive amount of whiskey consumed in a short time would swiftly destroy him. Every day for a week Malloy drank like a fish from noon to night, then staggered out into the dark. But instead of dying, he reappeared in Marino's each new day refreshed and ready for more.

A sense of urgency infected The Trust. Murphy, the former chemist, suggested that they start giving Malloy automobile antifreeze—wood alcohol—which is poisonous. The next day, when Malloy appeared on schedule, Murphy passed him a few straight shots of whiskey to soften him up for the lethal potion. Then came the antifreeze.

Malloy gulped it down without blinking, smacked his lips, and asked for a refill. A half-dozen shots were downed before Malloy passed out, collapsing to the floor at three in the morning. Pasqua examined him, said his heartbeat could hardly be heard and that he should be dead inside an hour. In three hours, however, Malloy sat up, apologized for his poor posture and said he was thirsty.

The men were astounded. For the next week, Malloy was poured double and triple shots, enough antifreeze to kill a battalion. At the end of each daily session he passed out, slept, woke up and asked for more.

Bewildered, Marino changed the formula. From now on Malloy must be given turpentine. The Irishman accepted it, swallowed glass after glass and stumbled out into the night. And, always, bounced back for more the following day. Soon turpentine was replaced by shots of undiluted horse liniment, sometimes lightened by rat poison. Malloy flourished.

The mood of The Murder Trust grew dark. Perhaps if Malloy could be fed some poisoned food from the free lunch table, that would do him in. Immediately, Murphy opened an old can of sardines and put it outside to spoil. When contamination was certain, he spread the sardines on a slice of bread, mixed in some carpet tacks and some metal shavings of the sardine can, laid on another piece of bread and presented it to Malloy. Delighted with the bartender's generosity, Malloy finished it all, then washed it down with more wood alcohol before starting home.

The conspirators were gleeful as they waited for word of Malloy's death. But the following morning brought no word. And the afternoon brought Malloy in person, ready for a drink and another sandwich!

This was too much. The gang began to regard Malloy as a phenomenon of nature. His stomach obviously was cast iron. If he were to be obliterated, another means must be found. They considered several and settled on the surefire one Marino had employed before.

Marino engaged the services of his friend Harry Green, 24, a cabbie, and on one of the coldest, snowiest nights of the winter, with an icy wind and a temperature that would dive close to zero, Malloy was encouraged to drink himself into a stupor. Marino and Pasqua then carried him to Green's taxi, waiting outside. Green drove them all to Crotona Park, where the coatless Malloy was laid out behind some bushes and doused with a five-gallon tin of water.

The next day, the gang eagerly searched the papers for news of Malloy's death. There was nothing. That evening, Pasqua showed up with a bad head cold from the outing the night before. Then the speakeasy door opened and there stood Michael Malloy, looking invigorated. He marched to the bar, calling out for his first drink.

Frantic, the men decided to call in a professional killer named Anthony "Tough Tony" Bastone. He advised them to stop the fancy stuff and just murder Malloy outright.

In the early hours of the next morning, once more using Green's taxi, Marino and Bastone drove to Baychester Avenue near Gun Hill Road. Malloy, who had passed out hours before, sat slumped between them. They dragged him out onto the deserted avenue and held him up. Green backed up his taxi, then catapulted it toward them at 45 m.p.h. Marino and Bastone released Malloy and jumped aside as the speeding auto smashed full into him, throwing him into the air, knocking him down, then running over him. Leaving the presumed corpse in the middle of the street, the satisfied trio fled.

Malloy did not appear the next day. A week passed and still no Malloy. The Murder Trust felt sure he was dead at last, but they had to prove it to the insurance companies. They read the obituaries. They visited the morgue. They phoned hospitals. No corpse.

Then, in the second week of Malloy's disappearance, the habitués of Marino's were thrown into turmoil. Michael Malloy himself walked in, apologizing for his absence. He'd been in a hospital (which had neglected to list him as a patient). A car accident, he explained: he'd suffered a concussion of the brain and a fractured shoulder. But now he was fine. "And I'm sure ready for a drink," he said.

Close to defeat, The Murder Trust decided to get rid of Malloy the quickest way possible, and risk be damned. On Washington's Birthday, the gang treated Malloy to his quota of drinks until he passed out. Kreisberg and Murphy took him to Murphy's room and dropped him on the bed. One end of a rubber hose was attached to a gas jet, the other end stuffed into Malloy's mouth. They let the gas fill him up.

In the morning, Michael Malloy was dead. Dr. Frank Manzella, an ex-alderman, wrote up a phony death certificate for The Trust, stating that Malloy had expired from lobar pneumonia. Pasqua placed Malloy in a $10 pine coffin and buried him in a $12 cemetery plot.

So, in the end, Malloy had lost. Yet not completely. Members of The Murder Trust grew suspicious of one another and they talked too much. The Bronx police began to hear rumors. When they learned that an actual Michael Malloy had died on Washington's Birthday, with three policies on his life, they had his body exhumed. The coroner found Malloy had been eliminated by use of illuminating gas, and members of The Trust were charged with murder. (But not "Tough Tony" Bastone, the hired killer: he was shot and killed in a money dispute before he could be indicted.)

The trial was held in Bronx County Court. The jury deliberated seven hours. Harry Green and Frank Manzella went to prison. On June 7, 1934, Anthony Marino, Frank Pasqua and Daniel Kreisberg went to the electric chair in Sing Sing. A month later Joseph Murphy also died in the chair.

Because of his indestructibility, Malloy had forced his killers to resort to obvious murder. As a result, four of them died. And they remain as dead today as ever. Yet, somehow, Michael Malloy lives.

Last of the Old-Time Shooting Sheriffs

by Cleveland Amory

When Uncle Jim Roberts came back home to the copper town of Jerome, he was 71—an old age for a hero. Jim was the last of Arizona's boom-town marshals, and quite possibly the best of them all. "I've seen better trick shots," said John Ryan, an old-time deputy, "but for plain ordinary business shooting, I'll take Jim Roberts."

Of course they couldn't give him his old job back; instead they gave him an honorary job as sheriff of Clarkdale, a little smelter town five miles away. A new one-block place, it was modern and law-abiding. Just to be on the safe side they took the Clarkdale bank off Jim's beat, assigning a separate younger guard to that.

Uncle Jim had nothing much to do except direct a little traffic. Most of the time he stayed at a post outside of Miller's Store. Wearing a plain white shirt, with a plain black hat, eastern size, clamped down on his head, Jim would lean back, chewing tobacco and whittling on a big stick. He always returned your greeting; question him, though, and he would shut up like a clam.

From the beginning, the old marshal was a big disappointment to the kids. He didn't look as if he had ever been a real shooting sheriff of the Old West. His eyes looked as if they needed glasses. He wasn't particularly strong and he wasn't particularly tall. He didn't drink or smoke or even play cards. He disliked swearing; "dang!" was his strongest expression. He didn't like riding horseback; when he had to go somewhere, he rode a mule. At home his wife thought of him not as a good man with a gun but as a good man around the house, one who liked her hot biscuits and who helped with the laundry.

Then there was the matter of his gun. The least the kids expected from a man of his reputation would have been two guns, but Jim only wore one, and old frontier-model single-action Colt that didn't look as if it had been shot for 20 years; and there were no notches on it. Worse still, Uncle Jim wore it loose in his side pocket without even a holster. That gun was the final straw. To the younger generation, Uncle Jim was more of a myth than a hero—until one day . . .

Judged in retrospect, Jim Roberts' previous life seems to have been a perfect buildup for that final showdown. He was born in Beaver, Mo., in 1856; nothing else is known of his early life until, at age 18, he arrived in central Arizona and settled in a cabin he built near the head of Tonto Creek. It was the wildest section of a wild and lonely land.

He brought with him a purebred stallion with an arched neck and a deep broad chest. He bred him with the tough, wiry range mares and soon young Jim Roberts, who didn't like to ride, became known for his horses. Then a few of these horses began to disappear.

There is no record that, at first, Roberts took any action. A little rustling was to be expected in that wild lawless region. But one day his prize stallion disappeared. This time Roberts determined to track his horse down. The trail led to the ranch of some people named Graham. Roberts made his accusations and possibly took stronger steps; no one knows. But one night he returned to find his little cabin home a pile of smoldering ashes.

Jim Roberts promptly declared war on the Grahams. This put him on one side of a feud which ranks as one of the bloodiest in American history—the Pleasant Valley War.

The fighting was intense. Legend has it that a band of Indians accidentally rode into the thick of one shooting affray. They were Apaches and on the warpath but they wanted no part of that kind of fighting and promptly fled.

Roberts developed two distinguishing traits as a gun-fighter. The first was that he scorned quick shooting; the other man could always get first shot. The second—well, it was that no opponent ever had a second shot. Old-timers said that among all the motley outlaws of the feud—the so-called "short-trigger men" from Texas, Billy the Kid's ex-gangsters from New Mexico—Roberts stood out as the most valuable fighting man. Zane Grey wrote a novel about the Pleasant Valley War which he called *To the Last Man*. Well, they say, Jim Roberts was the last man.

Roberts himself never discussed his role. One murder occurred four years after the feud was supposed to have been settled; it was believed to have been caused by loose talk reopening old sores. Afterward Roberts pledged his word never to talk.

The Pleasant Valley War left Roberts with a legendary reputation but little else. In 1890 he landed at Congress, a little gold and silver camp. But both ores were running out by the time he got there and he found neither; instead, he found a wife and a job.

They met at a dance. Her name was Permelia Kirkland. Her parents had been the first white couple married in the territory of Arizona. "Melia," 20 and blonde, was the belle of the town. Roberts asked her for a dance; he also gave her some lump candy. Two days later, in a black bow tie and a high-buttoned suit, Mr. Roberts came to call. Miss Kirkland was engaged to another at the time: "A nice boy, but he wasn't the man Jim was."

The job was at Jerome. As the last of the mining camps it was held in a death grip by ex-badmen from Virginia City, Tombstone and other points. Advised to handle its problem like other boom towns and choose a man with a name—western sense—to serve as peace officer, Jerome decided on Roberts. He accepted.

Married in Prescott on November 17, 1891, The Robertses left by stagecoach for Jerome next morning.

Jerome was a town of single men and saloons. The men worked underground ten hours a day, six days a week; the saloons worked 24 hours a day, seven days a week, behind thick stone shutters designed for keeping outside shootings out and inside shootings in. Mine paydays were every 30 days; the night after one, no one was safe on the streets.

Some recalled the marshal taking off up the mountain after a Mexican desperado, Roberts mounted on his favorite black mule, "Jack," and leading a little white burro to bring back the man's prospective corpse—which he did. In the years before the town had a jail, on the night after a payday Roberts often had what looked like half the population handcuffed—to posts, wagon wheels and wagons.

One old-timer remembered how he was broken in by Roberts as a young deputy. When three men had effected a gambling-table murder, they escaped to the outskirts of the town and sent a challenge to Roberts and his deputy to come and get them. "You take the middle fellow," said Roberts, as they approached the men, "and I'll get the front one and the other one." The young deputy's gun-hand began shaking. "Get out of the way, sonny," said the marshal kindly, "and I'll take 'em all." A moment later he did.

As for Roberts himself, he said almost as little of his experience at Jerome as he did of his experience in the Pleasant Valley War. "Jim never did say much," reported old Tom Jones, "and when he was mad he didn't say anything."

In June 1903 Roberts left Jerome and for 22 years served as marshal or sheriff of three other towns—Douglas, Florence and Humboldt. Then in 1927, at the age of 71, he took the job at Clarkdale.

It was late in that first year at Clarkdale that a movie company, on location for filming *To the Last Man*, came to town and asked Uncle Jim to be technical director, offering him a large salary—more money than he had made in his whole life.

The news went all over town. The kids were jubilant; their old marshal was real after all! Then, like a bolt from the blue, Uncle Jim had refused the offer. The movie company did not believe he was serious. There could be no reason to refuse to discuss the Pleasant Valley War now. According to the old-timers, all fighting participants of the feud except Roberts were dead. Uncle Jim said he was sorry but he still saw a reason: a man's word was something he kept until he himself died.

The movie company, by now as unbelieving as the kids, asked him to demonstrate how he had handled a gun. Surrounded by the men from Hollywood and all the Clarkdale kids, Uncle Jim obliged. He put down his whittling stick and slowly drew his gun. Arms extended, he held it straight out in front of him, both eyes open and both hands on the gun. He held the position several seconds. Then, without a word, Uncle Jim put his gun away, picked up his stick and went back to whittling.

It was enough for the men from Hollywood and enough for the kids from Clarkdale. Uncle Jim had as much as admitted that he was a myth. The crowd dissolved—and the curtain descended on Act Two of this real-life western.

Act Three opened at 11 o'clock on the morning of June 21, 1928. Into the Clarkdale branch of the Bank of Arizona strode two young men, Willard Forrester, 26, of Tulsa, Okla., and Earl Nelson, 22, of Wichita, Kan. Forrester wore gloves; Nelson wore a Colt automatic.

They were experienced operators. Working their way west from Wichita, they had racked up, in two short years, a long series of successful holdups. They planned one last big job and then a break to Mexico. A casing of Arizona convinced them that the sleepy little town of Clarkdale, with a mine payroll in its bank, was the best bet.

They had a car outside the bank, waiting for their getaway. They had three extra revolvers, a rifle, a shotgun and a riot gun. They and 47 cans of roofing nails to scatter over the road to block auto pursuit and, in case of having to leave their car, a large supply of ginger, cayenne pepper and oil of peppermint to rub on their shoes and foil pursuit by dogs. They had several days' food supply.

Nelson held up the bank personnel while Forrester disarmed them. Along with ten amazed customers, they were herded into the vault. Then, taking $50,000, the gunmen calmly locked the grill door of the vault and walked outside. Forrester climbed into the driver's seat, smiled to Nelson, and started up. They had engineered the biggest bank robbery in Arizona history.

There had been only one hitch in their plans. Unknown to

them, the bank manager, David Saunders, had managed to unlock the grill door by a trick catch, find a gun and was coming out after them.

Flushed with success, Forrester and Nelson started to tour confidently back through town. Just as they passed Jim Roberts' post at Miller's Store, Saunders, bravely running after them, fired two warning shots. Nelson leaned out of the car, shouted something, and took a pot shot at Uncle Jim.

He missed.

Uncle Jim put down his stick. As Saunders came running up, he spoke to him quietly. "Dang it, Dave," he said, "get down!" Then slowly, as he had demonstrated for Hollywood, he drew his gun. Both eyes open and both hands on the gun no one had seen him shoot in 20 years, he shot back—once. Fifty paces away in the fast-moving car, at a bad angle, Willard Forrester slumped over the wheel, a slug of lead in his brain.

The car careened around in a crazy circle, hit a telephone guy wire and smashed to rest against the Clarkdale High School. Earl Nelson jumped out and ran down the alley beside the building. Uncle Jim went after him—and there, in full view of at least some of the kids who had thought him a myth, the 72-year-old hero took his 22-year-old prisoner.

Uncle Jim was late for lunch that day and Mrs. Roberts was worried about her hot biscuits. "Jim said he was sorry, but he'd had a little trouble."

Six years after the robbery, on the evening of January 8, 1934, they found Uncle Jim at his post outside Miller's, lying on the ground; he had suffered a heart attack. A few minutes later, in an ambulance on his way to the hospital, he died—with his shoes on. According to the old-timers, Uncle Jim Roberts never did wear boots.

School Days

The Two Worlds of Sione
by Nardi Reeder Campion

In 1963, in the tiny Polynesian kingdom of Tonga—150 islands dotting 270 square miles in the vast South Pacific—a competitive exam was given to all high-school students. The Putney School, a small prep school in faraway Vermont, U.S.A., offered a scholarship to one of the high scorers, 16-year-old Sione Tupouniua. Within weeks he bade his parents, two sisters and six brothers a tearful good-by and sailed on the monthly passenger-freighter from his home island of Tongatapu to Fiji, where he boarded a plane.

Sione's plane arrived over San Francisco at night, and when the boy from Tonga saw the great blaze of light he thought the city was on fire. Dazzled, open-mouthed, he stepped down the gangway. His baggy gray suit was too big and very wrinkled. He had no idea how to tie a necktie, so he had wound it loosely about his neck. His bushy hair stood straight up, and he wore socks but no shoes. He had bought his first pair in Fiji—triple-E width, the widest made—but they proved so painful that now he simply carried them.

Transportation had been arranged to take Sione from the airport to a hotel. At the hotel, the youth tried to communicate. Although he had studied English, all he could say comfortably was "hello," "good-by," "please" and "thank you." The manager took one look at the gesticulating boy with the wild hair and moved rapidly to whisk him out of sight.

He shoved a key into Sione's hand, put him in the self-service elevator and told him to get off at the tenth floor. Sione's recollection of what happened next is vivid: "The door slid shut, the box went up, and I got airplane stomach again. Then the box stopped at the ninth floor. What to do? I figured, nine and one make ten, so if I push ONE I should go up to TEN."

He pushed ONE, and when the door opened he was back in the lobby. The manager shouted, "What are you doing down here?" He grabbed a bellboy and said, "Take this—er—gentleman up to his room, and put him *inside it*."

The bellboy smiled and Sione grinned back, relieved to find that Americans *could* smile. The bellboy showed Sione to his room, turned on the shower to warm the water, and left. It never occurred to him that a traveler might not know what a shower was, much less what "H" and "C" stood for.

Soon steam was everywhere, and the room became blistering hot. Sione took off his clothes; it felt good to be naked again. The steam seeped under the bedroom door and out into the hall. A man passing by saw it and rang the fire alarm. People came running into Sione's room, shouting. The manager shouted loudest of all, his face scarlet.

Sione just stood there, naked and speechless. The manager threw a towel at him and yelled, "For heaven's sake, cover yourself up!"

Firemen with helmets charged through the steam. Sione did not know what was going on; he supposed it was some strange American custom. One of the firemen discovered the shower running. He turned it off, and they all laughed—even the nervous manager. *We laughed together*, Sione remembers. *I felt good. In Tonga we laugh a lot. When you laugh with people, you're not strangers anymore.*

Sione rode east on the bus all the next day, popeyed with excitement, but weak from hunger. When the bus stopped, he eagerly followed a fellow passenger into a restaurant. The waitress placed a menu on his plate. In Tonga, banana leaves are used as plates, and extra leaves are placed on top to keep the food hot. Sione looked under the menu to see the food. Nothing. Then he tried to peel off the paper, thinking it might be something to eat. Finally, the waitress opened the menu for him, and he pointed at random.

Now Sione examined the silver and napkin, trying to figure out what to do with them. But when the waitress put a dish in front of him, he couldn't swallow one bite—it was a plate full of white worms! Weeks later he learned that this food was called spaghetti.

Outside the restaurant, Sione ran into a fruit vendor and bought oranges, bananas, a pineapple, a coconut. He smashed the coconut and began to pick out the meat. The other bus passengers gathered around to watch. Sione grinned and the others grinned back.

That's nice, he thought, *they're friendly. It's so sad to see all these people just sitting there, silent. At home, everyone would be joking and laughing and having a good time on a trip, whether they knew each other or not. In Tonga, we think it is rude not to talk, and politeness to strangers is instilled in us from childhood.*

When, at last, his bus pulled into Putney, where he was met by his American "parent," Edward Dodd, Sione was so exhausted he slept for 36 hours. When he awoke, 8000 miles from home, his strange situation struck him like a blow in the face, and tears started. Everything was so foreign. He didn't even dare use the bathroom: it was too clean. *In Tonga, most people simply went to an outhouse.*

Mr. and Mrs. Dodd did all they could to make their forlorn guest feel at home. They even held a pig roast for him, and introduced him to several boys his age. They helped him with his English, which quickly improved. They took him to his first church service in America. Sione eagerly looked forward to it. Methodist missionaries had converted the Tongans in the early 19th century, and religion is so important that even fishing is forbidden on Sunday. But Sione's first Sunday was sadly disappointing.

Only a handful of people were there. I thought the others were late, but they didn't come at all. Our church is packed every Sunday. Everybody wears white, and the service is full of joy. Here everybody wore black, and it was as if someone had died. The music made me homesick. I thought about the beautiful hymns my father composes, and I cried all during the service. We cry a lot at home. It helps you get rid of bad feelings; then you get up and go on. The Bible says Jesus wept—why should American men be embarrassed to cry?

When Putney opened, the other students were puzzled by the new boy's woebegone expression and odd ways. Luckily, however, there was a soccer game that first week. Sione had never seen soccer, but like most Tongans, he is a natural athlete and was the star of the game—even in his bare feet. From then on, all the students felt warmer toward him, and his feelings of strangeness started to dissolve. Soon Sione's sense of humor and natural openness made him many friends.

Those first months in the United States were booby-trapped with strange devices, like clocks *(My mother would tell us, "Try to be home by the time the sun gets below the mango tree")* and locks *(If someone wants something badly enough to steal, we say let him have it)*. The feeling of isolation was hardest to adjust to. Privacy is unknown in the open houses and grass huts of Tonga; in the United States, people seem to prefer going it alone. *Here, helping others is only an obligation. In Tonga, helping others is the joy that gives life its meaning.*

The greatest thrill in Sione's new life came from learning. He had always taken the Tongan school lightly, often skipping classes altogether to swim or fish. Now, all at once, the world of the mind was open to him. He learned quickly, and the excitement of learning propelled him into more learning.

Everything I was exposed to was new. The discovery of the test tube and the microscope and history and maps and typewriters and films and all those books was so sudden for me. I read, read all the time. Only two books have been published in Tongan—the Bible and a hymnal. Now I could read book after book in English! I began with Melville's stories of my own South Seas, and kept going. American kids have grown up with the tools of knowledge, so the excitement of discovery escapes them. The trouble with being sophisticated is that you lose the joy of surprise.

This adventure in learning was remarkably successful: after two years at Putney, Sione Tupouniua of Tonga sailed into Harvard College with a full scholarship. There he was an honors student, on the dean's list, president of his club, and captain of the varsity rugby team. Summers he spent working as a carpenter. "Sione's natural joyousness inspires the others here," said a Harvard housemaster. "Without even knowing it, he seeds this place with ideas of how to live."

Many things in America still puzzled Sione. He did not understand young people's lack of respect for their elders; nor their love of loud music that prevents communication; nor their fear of getting fat. (Tongans admire great weight. King Tupou IV is envied because he weighs 300 pounds.)

Some aspects of student social life bothered Sione. *American boys and girls get too serious too soon. They start thinking ahead instead of rejoicing in the present. And I don't understand the continuous debate about morality. To us, morality is not how much of the body is covered up or how much joy you deny yourself. Morality is how you treat people. If you are kind and loving to them, that is moral. If you are mean and selfish to them, that is immoral.*

After Harvard, Sione went on to Oxford University. Then back to Fiji, where he taught political science and economics at the South Pacific University while completing work on his doctoral thesis. His plan was to return to Tonga to live. He would like to start a college. (There is none there now.) He doesn't want Tongans to lose their loving, natural ways; but he would like to pass on to them some of America's ability to counter the destructive forces of nature: weather, insects, disease. He hopes to help them share American know-how—the experience of organizing difficult jobs and getting them done.

While still in the U.S.A. Sione said: *Back in Tonga I know I will miss books and libraries; films, plays and concerts; the change of seasons; snow and the thrill of skiing; and, most of all, friends. I don't think I'll miss modern conveniences and physical comforts, like television and hot baths, and I know I won't miss the uncomfortable clothes, the crowds, the noise, the polluted air, the traffic jams, and the people who half-run, half-walk.*

I have a goal: to give my people a deep appreciation of what we have in Tonga—something you can discover only by going away. We have nothing, really, and yet we have so much. We have ofa. "Ofa" is a Tongan word meaning respect, kindness, sympathy and love—all the things of the heart. It is the most important word in our vocabulary. In America, success is measured by what you produce or what you possess. In Tonga, success is measured only in terms of your relationships with other human beings.

"A Troublesome Boy"

by *Winston S. Churchill*

I was on the whole considerably discouraged by my school days. All my contemporaries seemed in every way better adapted to the conditions of our little world. They were far better both at the games and at the lessons. It is not pleasant to feel oneself completely left behind at the very beginning of the race.

I was first threatened with school when I was seven years old. At the time I was what grown-up people in their offhand way called "a troublesome boy." Although much that I had heard about school had made a disagreeable impression on my mind, an impression thoroughly borne out by the actual experience, I thought it would be fun to go away and live with so many other boys, and that we should have great adventures. Also I was told that "school days were the happiest time in one's life." All the boys enjoyed it. Some of my cousins had been quite sorry—I was told—to come home for the holidays.

Cross-examined, the cousins did not confirm this; they only grinned.

It was a dark November afternoon when the last sound of my mother's departing carriage died away and I was taken into a Form Room and told to sit at a desk. All the other boys were out of doors and I was alone with the Form Master. He produced a thin, greeny-brown-covered book.

"This is a Latin grammar." He opened it at a well-thumbed page. "You must learn this," he said, pointing to several words in a frame of lines. "I will come back in half an hour and see what you know."

Behold me then on a gloomy evening, with an aching heart, seated in front of the declension of *mensa*.

What on earth did it mean? It seemed absolute rigmarole to me. However, there was one thing I could always do: I could learn by heart.

In due course the Master returned.

"Have you learned it?" he asked.

"I think I can *say* it, sir," I replied; and I gabbled it off.

He seemed so satisfied with this that I was emboldened to ask a question.

"What does it mean, sir?"

"It means what it says. *Mensa*, a table."

"Then why does *mensa* also mean O table," I inquired, "and what does O table mean?"

"*Mensa*, O table, is the vocative case," he replied. "You would use that in speaking to a table."

"But I never do," I blurted out in honest amazement.

Such was my first introduction to the classics from which, I have been told, many of our cleverest men have derived so much solace and profit.

Flogging with the birch was a great feature in the curriculum. Two or three times a month the whole school was marshaled in the Library, and one or more delinquents were haled off to an adjoining apartment and there flogged until they bled freely, while the rest sat quaking, listening to their screams. How I hated this school and what a life of anxiety I lived there for more than two years! I made very little progress at my lessons and none at all at games. The greatest pleasure I had was reading. When I was nine and a half my father gave me *Treasure Island*, and I remember the delight with which I

devoured it. My teachers saw me at once backward and pre-
cocious, reading books beyond my years and yet at the bottom
of the Form. They were offended. They had large resources
of compulsion at their disposal, but I was stubborn.

Where my reason, imagination or interest was not engaged,
I would not or I could not learn. In all the 12 years I was at
school no one ever succeeded in making me write a Latin verse
or learn any Greek except the alphabet. To stimulate my flag-
ging interest they told me that Mr. Gladstone read Homer for
fun, which I thought served him right.

I had scarcely passed my 12th birthday when I entered the
inhospitable regions of examinations. These were a great trial
to me. The subjects which were dearest to the examiners were
almost invariably those I fancied least. I would have liked to
have been examined in history, poetry and writing essays. The
examiners, on the other hand, were partial to Latin and mathematics. Moreover, I should have liked to be asked to say what
I knew. They always tried to ask what I did not know. When
I would have willingly displayed my knowledge, they sought
to expose my ignorance. This sort of treatment had only one
result: I did not do well in examinations.

This was especially true of my entrance examination to
Harrow. The Headmaster, Dr. Welldon, however, took a
broad-minded view of my Latin prose; he showed discernment
in judging my general ability. This was remarkable because
I was found unable to answer a single question in the Latin
paper. I wrote my name at the top of the page. I wrote down
the number of the question: I. After much reflection I put a
bracket round it thus: (I). But thereafter I could not think of
anything connected with it that was either relevant or true.
Incidentally there arrived from nowhere in particular a blot and
several smudges. I gazed for two whole hours at this sad spectacle and then merciful ushers collected my piece of foolscap.
It was from these slender indications of scholarship that Dr.
Welldon drew the conclusion that I was worthy to pass into
Harrow. It is very much to his credit. It showed that he was
a man capable of looking beneath the surface of things: a man
not dependent upon paper manifestations. I have always had
the greatest regard for him.

I was in due course placed in the lowest division of the
bottom Form. I continued in this unpretentious situation for

nearly a year. However, by being so long in the lowest Form I gained an immense advantage over the cleverer boys. They all went on to learn Latin and Greek and splendid things like that. But I was taught English. We were considered such dunces that we could learn only English. As I remained in the Third Fourth three times as long as anyone else, I had three times as much of it. I learned it thoroughly. Thus I got into my bones the essential structure of the ordinary British sentence—which is a noble thing. And when in after years my schoolfellows who had won prizes and distinction for writing such beautiful Latin poetry and pithy Greek epigrams had to come down again to common English to earn their living or make their way, I did not feel myself at any disadvantage.

It was thought incongruous that, while I apparently stagnated in the lowest Form, I should gain a prize open to the whole school for reciting to the Headmaster 1200 lines of Macaulay's "Lays of Ancient Rome" without making a single mistake. I also succeeded in passing the preliminary examination for the Army while many boys far above me failed in it. I also had a piece of good luck. We knew that among other questions we should be asked to draw from memory a map of some country or other. The night before, by way of final preparation, I put the names of all the maps in the atlas into a hat and drew out New Zealand. I applied my good memory to the geography of that Dominion. Sure enough the first question in the paper was: "Draw a map of New Zealand." Henceforward all my education was directed in the Army class to passing into Sandhurst. Officially I never got out of the Lower School at Harrow.

It took me three tries to pass into Sandhurst. There were five subjects, of which Mathematics, Latin and English were obligatory, and I chose in addition French and Chemistry. In this hand I held only a pair of Kings—English and Chemistry. Nothing less than three would open the jackpot. I had to find another useful card. Latin I could not learn. French was interesting but rather tricky. So there remained only Mathematics. I turned to them—I turned on them—in desperation.

Of course what I call Mathematics is only what the Civil Service Commissioners expected you to know to pass a very rudimentary examination. Nevertheless, when I plunged in I was soon out of my depth. I was soon in a strange corridor of things called Sines, Cosines and Tangents. Apparently they were very important, especially when multiplied by each other or by themselves! They had also this merit—you could learn many of their evolutions off by heart. There was a question in my third and last examination about these Cosines and Tangents in a highly square-rooted condition which must have been decisive upon the whole of my after life. But luckily I had seen its ugly face only a few days before and recognized it at first sight.

I have never met any of these creatures since. With my third and successful examination they passed away like the phantasmagoria of a fevered dream. I am assured that they are most helpful in engineering, astronomy and things like that. I am glad there are quite a number of people born with a gift and a liking for all of this; like great chess players, for example, who play 16 games at once blindfold and die quite soon of epilepsy.

The practical point is that, if I had not been asked this particular question about these Cosines or Tangents, I might have gone into the Church and preached orthodox sermons in a spirit of audacious contradiction to the age. I might have gone into the City and made a fortune. I might even have gravitated to the Bar and persons might have been hanged through my defense who now nurse their guilty secrets with complacency.

In retrospect my school years form the only barren and unhappy period of my life. Actually, no doubt, they were buoyed up by the laughter and high spirits of youth. But I would far rather have been apprenticed as a bricklayer's mate or run errands as a messenger boy. It would have been real; it would have been natural; it would have taught me more; and I should have done it much better.

I am all for the Public Schools but I do not want to go there again.

The Washed Window

by Dorothy Canfield Fisher

You may never have noticed it: it used to be the last house you pass as you leave Arlington, Vt., to drive to Cambridge. But once, about 65 years ago, a great American educator who chanced to pass through Vermont asked to be shown that house. When he stood in front of the low old building he took off his hat and bowed his gray head in silence. "For me it is a shrine," he explained.

This is the story behind that visit. It goes back to the heart-shaking years of the Civil War, which left in the South thousands of newly emancipated blacks, free, but ignorant not only of their letters but of the simplest ways of civilized life. Many of the first schools for them were taught by Northern girls, and among these was young Viola Knapp, the schoolteacher daughter of Silas Knapp the cabinetmaker who built and lived in that small Arlington, Vt., house. To the accompaniment of great anxiety from her family, she made the difficult trip down South to one of the newly established schools for illiterate blacks.

When she arrived at the rough, improvised little school, Viola Knapp found that she was regarded as a social outcast by all the white people in town. No one spoke to her, no one even looked at her. She had great difficulty in finding a place to live, and finally moved into a tumble-down two-room abandoned frame house.

One would have thought that a blooming young woman in her 20's, away from home for the first time, would have suffered a good deal from this. But she was from Vermont, and wasn't too much cast down by disapproval if she herself felt sure she was doing the right thing.

But evidently what most helped her was her liking for another person who was being ostracized in the same way. This was young Lieutenant Ruffner of the U.S. Army, stationed there to care for the federal military cemetery. The acquaintance soon became an engagement, and after a while they were married. It turned out a happy, lifelong mating. The young lieutenant became a general, and our Vermont Viola had a much more colorful and wide-horizoned life than she would have had if she had not gone a-crusading.

The story I'm setting down here is about as I heard it from the lips of the distinguished American educator, who as a boy had been a student of Viola Knapp Ruffner.

I never knew exactly how old I was when I first saw Mrs. Ruffner. But from what I have been able to learn, I was born, a slave, on a Virginia plantation about 1858. My home had been a log cabin with a dirt floor about 14 by 16 feet square. We slept on piles of filthy rags. Until I was quite a big youth I wore only one garment, a shirt made of rough refuse flax.

We slaves ate corn bread and pork, because that could be grown on the plantation without cash expense. I had never seen anything except the slave quarters on the plantation where I was born, with a few glimpses of the "big house" where our white owners lived. I cannot remember ever, during my childhood and youth, one single time when our family sat down together at a table to eat a meal as human families do. We ate as animals do, whenever and wherever an edible morsel was found.

After the Civil War, when we were no longer slaves, my

family moved to a settlement near a salt mine, where, although I was still only a child, I was employed—often beginning my day's work at four in the morning. We lived in even more dreadful squalor there, for our poor rickety cabin was in a crowded slum, foul with unspeakable dirt—literal and moral. As soon as I grew a little older and stronger, I was shifted from the salt mine to a coal mine. Both mines were owned by General Lewis Ruffner.

By that time I had learned my letters and could, after a fashion, read; mostly I taught myself, with some irregular hours spent in a Negro night school. And I heard two pieces of news which were like very distant glimmers in the blackness of the coal mine. One was about a school for colored students— Hampton Institute, it was —where they could learn more than their letters. The other was that the wife of General Ruffner was from Vermont, that before her marriage she had been a teacher in one of the first schools for Negroes, and that she took an interest in the education of the colored people who worked for her.

I also heard she was so strict that nobody could suit her, and the colored boys who entered her service were so afraid of her and found her so impossible to please that they never stayed long. But the pay was five dollars a month and keep. And then there was the chance she might be willing to have me go on learning. I got up my courage to try.

Even though I was a great, lumbering, coal-mining boy, I was trembling when I went to ask for that work. The Ruffners had just moved into an old house that had been empty for some time and their furniture was not unpacked, the outbuildings not repaired. Mrs. Ruffner was writing on an improvised desk which was a plank laid across two kegs.

I falteringly told her I had come to ask for work. She turned in her chair and looked at me silently. Nobody had ever looked at me like that, as if she wanted to see what kind of person I was. She had clear, steady gray eyes, I remember. Then she said, "You can try. You might as well start in by cleaning the woodshed."

The woodshed was dark and cluttered with all kinds of dirty things; a sour smell came up from them. Mrs. Ruffner brought out a dustpan and a broom, put a shovel in my hand and said, "Now go ahead. Put the trash you clean out on that pile in the yard and we'll burn it up later. Anything that won't burn, like broken glass, put into that barrel." Then she left me.

You must remember that I had never cleaned a room in my life. I had never seen a clean room. But I was used to doing as I was told and dead set on managing to learn more. So I began taking out things which anybody could see were trash, like mildewed rags, which fell apart the minute I touched them. In one corner was the carcass of a long-dead dog, which I carried out to the pile of trash in the side yard. Glass was everywhere, broken whisky bottles, bits of crockery. These I swept with the broom and, picking up my sweepings in my hands (I had no idea what a dustpan was for), carried them outside.

The shed looked to me so much better that I went to find Mrs. Ruffner. She was still writing. I told her, "I cleaned it." Pushing back her chair, she went out to the woodshed with me.

She made no comment when she first opened the door and looked around her. Then she remarked quietly, "There's still some things to attend to. Those pieces of wood over there you might pile up against the wall in the corner. They would do to burn. Be sure to clean the floor well before you start piling the wood on it. And here's another pile of rotten rags, you see. And that tangle behind the door. You'd better pull it all apart and see what's there. Throw away the thrash that's mixed with it." She turned to go, saying, "Just keep on till you've got it finished and then come and tell me."

She didn't speak kindly. She didn't speak unkindly. I looked at the woodshed with new eyes and saw that I'd only made a beginning. And to my astonishment I saw I was perspiring.

The work wasn't hard for me, you understand. It was like little boy's play compared to the backbreaking labor I had always done. What made me sweat was the work I had to do with my mind. Always before, when somebody had given me a piece of work to do he had stood right there to do all the thinking for me.

I was determined to do it right this time. Now that I was really thinking about what I was doing, I was amazed how much more there was to do than I had seen.

I stooped to pull apart the mud-colored tangle heaped up back of the door. As I stirred it, a snake crawled out and wriggled toward the door. A big fellow. I wasn't surprised. I was used to snakes. I dropped a stone on his head and carried his long, black body out to the trash pile.

Now I had come to a corner where chickens had evidently roosted; everything was covered with their droppings. I thought nothing of handling them, nor of taking up the body of one chicken I found lying dead in the midst of the rubbish. More rotted rags, a stained, torn pair of pants, too far gone even for me to wear. Some pieces of wood fit for fuel. Everything had first to be pulled loose from the things it was mixed up with, and I had to think what to do with it. No wonder that the sweat ran down my face so that, to see, I had to wipe my eyes with the back of my hands.

Finally, the last of the refuse was cleared away and the filth which had dropped from it to the floor as I worked was swept together and carried out to the trash pile. I went in to get Mrs. Ruffner. "I got it done," I told her.

Laying down her pen, she came again to see. I felt nervous as, silent and attentive, she ran those clear eyes of hers over what I had been doing. But I wasn't prepared to have her say again, "That's better, but there's a great deal still to do. You haven't touched the cobwebs."

I looked up at them; my lower jaw dropped. Sure enough, they hung in long, black festoons. I had not once lifted my head to see them. "And how about washing the windows? Get a pail of water for that. Here are some clean rags. You'll have to go over it several times."

She went back into the house and I stood shaken by more new ideas than I could tell you about. I hadn't even noticed there was a window, it was so thick with dust and cobwebs. I had never had anything to do with a glass window. In the dark cabins I had lived in, the windows were just holes cut in the walls.

I set to work once more, the sweat running down my face. Suppose she wouldn't even let me try to do her work? I never could get into Hampton. What if I just never could get the hang of her ways? I began again to clean that woodshed! Once in a while I stopped stock-still to *look* at it, as I had never looked at anything before, trying really to see it. I don't know that I ever in my life afterward cared about doing anything right as much as getting that little old woodshed clean.

When I came to what I thought was the end, I looked up at the slanting roof; the rafters were not only cleared of cobwebs but bare of dust. The floor was swept clean: not a chip, not a thread, not a glint of broken glass on it. Piles of firewood against the walls. And the window! I had washed that window five times! How it sparkled. How the strong sunshine poured through it. The woodshed was a room. To me it looked like a parlor. I was proud of it. I had never been proud of anything I had done until then.

Then for the third time I went to call Mrs. Ruffner to inspect. Big boy as I was, twice her size, my hands were shaking, my lips twitching. I felt sick. Had I done it right this time? Could I ever do anything right?

I watched her face as she passed my work in review, looking carefully up, down and around. Then she turned to me and, looking straight into my eyes, she nodded and said, "Now it's clean. Nobody could have done it any better."

She had opened the door through which I took my first step toward civilized living.

The distinguished American who told me that story was Booker T. Washington, founder and longtime president of Tuskegee Institute.

First Love

by Lawrance Thompson

The poet Robert Frost frequently told me about his first love. She was, he said, a dark-haired, dark-eyed, mischievous tomboy. Her name was Sabra Peabody and she and Frost had been schoolmates, many years before, in Salem, N.H. As an awkward 12-year-old he wrote her ardent notes, but the young lady had many other admirers and did not encourage him. Eventually he moved away from the village and heard no more from her.

As Frost's official biographer, I mentally filed this information. But I did nothing about it until years later, when I heard that the same Sabra Peabody, now a widow, had returned to Salem to live. I wrote for an interview and received a cordial invitation from her to come to call.

I was received by a tall, lithe, vibrant woman in her 70's, white-haired, and still beautiful. Her memories about the school days with Frost were much like those the elderly poet had given me. She told me how she, her brother Charles and

"Rob" used to roam the woods together after school and on Saturdays. Adventurous like her brother, she used to tease Frost into keeping pace with them. She recalled that he sometimes quarreled with her over her other beaux.

I did not stay long that day, but was encouraged to return. It was during my second visit that the unexpected happened— the kind of thing biographers dream of but seldom encounter.

We had talked again, even more freely than before. Finally I stood to take my leave. Sabra remained seated. "Was there something else?" I asked. Yes, said Sabra, she had just been waiting for the right moment. She told me that this house, to which she had returned after her husband's death, had been her childhood home. Recently she had opened a dusty steamer trunk in the attic and found several family keepsakes, among them a wooden pencil box she had used in grammar-school days.

Holding it in her hand, she had suddenly remembered that in the bottom of the box there was a secret compartment which could be opened by sliding the thin wooden base outward. She tried it, the secret compartment opened, and out fell four notes, notes written by "Rob" to Sabra, perhaps in the fall of 1886. She now wanted me to see them.

As she took the notes out of a desk drawer and gave them to me, I felt great excitement in the knowledge that, almost by accident, I held the earliest known writing of a major literary figure. But as I began to read I found further rewards. "I like those leavs you gave me and put them in my speller to press," one note started out. Another pleaded: "There is no fun in getting mad every so often so lets see if we cant keep friends. . . . I like you because I cant help myself and when I get mad at you I feel mad at myself to." In such lines I could sense the rapture and the anguish of a boy in love.

The former Sabra Peabody had no idea of the importance of this find. When she offered to give me the notes, I explained that their market value was too high for me to accept them as a gift. But would she consider donating them to the collection of Robert Frost's papers at the Jones Public Library in Amherst, Mass.?"

She agreed, and I delivered them a few days later to Charles R. Green, curator of the collection. Since I feared that the poet might not approve of my snooping, I asked that this gift be

kept a secret. I further requested that the notes be matted, with
backing, and wrapped in heavy paper; that the package be tied
with string, and placed in the vault of the library with the
notation "Not to Be Opened During Robert Frost's Lifetime."
The secret might have been preserved as planned, had not fate
intervened—in the person of Robert Frost himself!

Frost had stored in that same vault a small metal strongbox
containing manuscripts of some early poems. Shortly after the
four notes had been turned over to the library, he appeared
there unexpectedly to retrieve one of the poems. Green offered
to bring the box out, but Frost said time could be saved if they
both went into the vault. The poet opened his strongbox, took
what he wanted, closed it—and looked around. "What's this?"
he asked.

Green had inadvertently placed the secret package on a
nearby shelf. Frost peered at it, then read aloud, "Not to Be
Opened During Robert Frost's Lifetime." He turned accusingly
to the curator. "This is your handwriting, Mr. Green."

Flustered, Green said yes, yes it was, but Larry Thompson
had asked him to write it because . . .

Frost was in no mood for explanations. With clenched hands
he broke the string, then tore the wrapping off the package.
After reading the notes carefully, the old gentleman shoved the
material back on the shelf. Then he turned and, without a word
to anyone, stalked out of the library.

Green's letter of apology gave me all the deatils and said
that the poet seemed very angry. I was worried. If Frost should
not forgive me for my snooping without his permission, my
work on the biography might end before it really began. What
could I do to make amends? Perhaps it would be best, I decided,
to let his anger cool, even to wait until *he* chose to bring up
the subject. I waited.

Nothing happened until the following June when I arrived
in Vermont to spend some time with the poet as he and I had
planned. When I reached his farm, he was in his vegetable
garden setting out a row of lettuce seedlings. His greeting was
cordial and his instructions were sensible: I should take off my
city jacket and prove my farming background by helping him
get these plants into the ground before they began to wilt. After
we finished, we went up to his cabin and sat down before the
stone fireplace. Frost began to tell me how a fox had made off

with one of his hens. "I didn't react fast enough," he said. "Nothing like that has happened to me since I was a boy in Salem and . . ."

Salem! Reminded of unfinished business, he stopped in the middle of the sentence. His expression changed. He leaned toward me, shook the index finger of his right hand under my nose, and said, "You! You! What *you* did to *me*!" With that he launched into his version of the visit to the Jones Library.

He said that as soon as he saw the admonition on the packet and heard Green say my name, he knew that I'd been prying. Hurt and angry that I hadn't confided in him, he had broken the string and torn open the package almost before he realized what he was doing.

The feeling of resentment had been swept away by the opening words: "Dear Sabe." No one could possibly understand, he said, how overwhelmed he was by the memories which flooded up as he read. By the time he finished the last note, he could feel the tears burning in his eyes. He couldn't bear to have Green see those tears; he couldn't talk to anyone. So he fled. When Frost paused and silence filled the room, I was the one whose eyes stung.

Then, suddenly, his manner changed and he looked me straight in the eye. "So you found her?" he asked quietly.

I nodded.

"Where?"

"Salem."

He continued to stare at me and I didn't dare go on. The silence became uncomfortable. Finally he spoke, almost to himself. "Sixty years!" I had to lean forward to hear him. "Sixty years . . . and I've never forgotten."

Then he leaned back. "You can start," he said quietly. "Start at the beginning and tell me all about her."

ONE of a Kind

The Lives and Loves of the Siamese Twins

by J.P. McEvoy

All of us have heard about the original Siamese twins, but how many of us could answer such questions as: were they legally two individuals or a partnership? If one committed a crime was the other a party to it? Did they get hungry and sleepy at the same time? How did they get along with each other? Which died first and why? How many widows were there? And how many children did they leave?

To begin with, Chang and Eng, later known as Chang-Eng Bunker (after a New York lady who treated them kindly), were born in 1811 in a tiny fishing village on the Mekong River not far from Bangkok, Siam. Their father was Chinese and their mother half Chinese, which made them only one quarter Siamese—or, to be quizzical, one eighth Siamese apiece.

They grew to the height of five feet one inch for Chang and five feet two inches for Eng (Chang wore special lifts in his shoes so his twin wouldn't top him) and they made themselves useful raising ducks and peddling eggs—and everyone re-marked how smart they were at driving bargains, for they both talked together, each finishing the other's sentence, and the ordinary haggler was no match for them.

One day, when the twins were 18 years old, a Yankee skipper dropped anchor in the harbor and accidentally met the twins. He immediately shanghaied them and brought them to Boston. They created a sensation, not only around Boston but in Europe where their protector next journeyed with them. We are told he toured 2500 miles in the British Isles alone, ex-hibiting the Twins to 300,000 Britishers. Even the august Royal College of Surgeons invited the twins to tea, and after discreetly examining them pronounced them "an extraordinary *Lusus Naturae.*"

They were all of that. Joined as they were, "they could run and swim, take walks of eight and ten miles, play battledore and shuttlecock, and on many occasions went hunting." They could walk only side by side. They slept face to face, changing positions by the simple expedient of rolling over, which they learned to do automatically without awakening each other. They were normal in every way except for a small, flexible band three and a half inches long and some eight inches in circumference connecting them from the extremity of the breast bone of each and extending downward to the abdomen.

There was a great difference of opinion among medical experts of the time concerning what went on inside this con-necting band and they never did find out until the postmortem, which was a world event, but all agreed that surgical divorce would have proved fatal. Meanwhile, it was an intriguing fact that a pinprick in the exact center of the "band" was felt by both twins but a puncture to the right or left was felt only by the twin nearer the injury. As children the twins contracted measles and smallpox at the same time and recovered simul-taneously, but as adults one twin was a periodic souse while the other was a complete teetotaler—and the alcoholic ecstasy of the one brother in no way affected the pious sobriety of the other.

They came back to America from their first trip, richer only in experience, the skipper having skipped (with the booty). But the twins, of age now, made other connections, including the immortal Barnum—with whom "they sojourned in New York

City for five years at the corner of Anne Street and Broadway (The American Museum)"—and finally accumulated an estate of $60,000.

Now if you were a Siamese twin you might think romance was not for you. Certain baffling complications and situations would of necessity arise to give you pause. So the Siamese twins must have thought—and then they had a most curious experience. In London a Miss Sophia, a young lady of "respectable connections," fell violently in love with both twins— to their mutual consternation. Unhappily she found, in the delicate prose of the day, "insurmountable impediments in her path—for the twins had been pronounced distinct individuals by eminent British medical men, and had her passion been fully returned she would scarcely have been disposed to encounter the risk of defending an action for bigamy which might naturally follow such a marriage." Thwarted and tormented by these unfeeling legal quibblers, Miss Sophia turned to the poets for comfort, selecting a poignant, and pertinent, couplet to bid them farewell:

> How happy could I be with either
> Were tother dear charmer away.

The twins provided plenty of legal puzzles for our own American lawyers, who used to argue about whether they could own property as individuals. Weren't they inevitably partners in ownership as in life? It was finally legally decided that they could hold property and sign contracts either as individuals or as joint partners, one signing for the other, but they must marry as individuals and their children would inherit separately.

But if one committed a crime, which would be guilty? Could the other be tried as an accessory? And if one was innocent how could you punish or imprison the other without making the innocent party suffer? No one could argue lack of knowledge on the part of the other—for the twins always fell asleep at the same time, woke up at the same time, were hungry simultaneously, ate the same food in similar quantities, each smoked and chewed tobacco when the other did, and though many people had tried, it had been proved impossible to engage the two of them in separate conversations or on different subjects. While they disagreed violently about many things they could talk only on the same subject at the same time—each finishing the other's sentence as in childhood.

Curiously enough, they seldom spoke to each other. They explained this once by saying they both saw the same things at the same time and felt the same way about them so there was nothing to discuss. For the same reason they disliked playing games in which they were pitted against each other, such as chess—at which they were quite good—explaining they took no more pleasure playing competitively "than you would in playing your right hand against your left." Politics was something else again. During a local Congressional election in 1847 they differed so violently that they voted for different candidates.

For by now these three-fourths Chinese were American citizens, by special act of the Legislature of North Carolina. They had learned to speak English pretty well, to read and write. They had adopted American dress except that each wore his hair in a queue (old Chinese style) three and a half feet long, wrapped tightly around his head. They were prosperous farmers, too.

Somewhere in their travels the twins had another romantic adventure. This time two sisters fell in love with them. Contemporary meanies were ungallant enough to say the $60,000 estate had something to do with it. Anyway, on April 1, 1843, in Wilkes County, North Carolina, Chang married Adelaide Yeats and Eng married her sister, Sarah Ann—and we would like to add that they lived together happily ever after, but they didn't. For the sisters didn't get along and the brothers weren't too congenial about their sisters-in-law. A working solution was finally arrived at—the twins built separate houses for their wives three miles apart near Mount Airy, N.C., and lived three days at a time in each house—a design for living that intrigued the countryside.

The twins were married for more than 30 years and between them had a total of 22 children, all exceptionally bright. Eng was the champ, with seven boys and five girls—all normal. Chang had seven girls and three boys—and they, too, were normal except that one boy and one girl were deaf-mutes.

The Civil War came along and the twins, sympathetic to the Confederacy, shared its defeat. Impoverished, they came to New York to recoup their finances and exhibited at Wood's

Museum, but the public had lost interest. Despondent, neglected, they faded out of public view and spent their last days on their farms—faithfully going back and forth to each other's house every three days regardless of the weather.

Some of the old chronicles say this was the death of them—that Chang caught a severe cold riding in the rain. Other accounts have it that Chang went on one alcoholic spree too many. In any case, on Friday evening, January 23, 1874, in the sixty-third year of their amazing lives, they retired to a small room by themselves and went to bed. But Chang was restless. Sometime between midnight and daybreak they got up and sat by the fire in a special chair which had been made for them. Eng was sleepy and wanted to go to bed. Chang complained that it hurt his chest to lie down. They argued about it while Eng smoked his pipe. Finally Eng knocked out his pipe and they went to bed, and Eng fell into a deep sleep.

And now the curtain—surely as macabre a scene as was ever conceived:

"Eng waked up and asked his son, 'How is your Uncle Chang?' The boy said, 'Uncle Chang is cold. Uncle Chang is dead.' Then great excitement took place. Eng commenced crying, saying to his wife, whom they called in, 'My last hour has come.' As he turned in alarm to the lifeless form by his side he was seized with violent nervous paroxysms. In two hours he was dead, although he had been in perfect health when they went to bed."

The autopsy, held at a special meeting at the College of Physicians in Philadelphia, settled a number of questions for the medical world with words like teratology, omphalopagus Xiphodidymus, and duplex bilaterality. It also showed that any attempt to separate the twins in life would have been fatal. It showed that Chang died of a cerebral clot. But no cause could be found for the death of Eng. It was generally believed he died of fright.

MikE ANd His "WEAlty, PrrromiNENT" FriENds

by Betty MacDonald

I'm sure no woman ever enjoyed the attentions of a more lovable or more unusual suitor than Mike Gordon. Instead of flowers or candy, Mike would send me such gifts as a side of beef; 24 boxes of apples; four dozen pairs of nylons, slightly irregular as to size and color; 288 cans of split-pea soup; six handmade Tyrolean sweaters all exactly alike and all the wrong size; 200 ears of corn; a dozen hams; 367 bars of scented soap.

The stone that dislodged this avalanche of gifts was a casual introduction at a lunch. Even though I had been married and divorced and had two children, I was only 26 at the time; and since Mike was somewhere between 70 and 100, it never occurred to me that he would consider himself my suitor and would endeavor during the next eight years to out-suit anyone else.

Mike looked like a jolly little troll. He was not quite five feet tall, had a slight fringe of yellowish-white hair, small sparkling blue eyes, fat red cheeks, and a round little stomach always liberally sprinkled with cigarette ashes. He spoke with an odd accent which bore traces of Swedish, Scotch, Greek and dead-end kid.

Mike and I discovered that we were both from Butte, Montana, on that first day at lunch while our mutual friend was getting his coat. I lived with my mother and sisters in Seattle then, and I asked Mike if he had always lived in the state of Washington. He said he was originally from Butte, and I told him my father had been a mining engineer and my family had also lived there.

When our friend came back Mike calmly said, to my amazement, "I've known Betty since she was a baby. Knew her mudder and fadder well. Very wealty and prrrominent man." I found out later that Mike was like a child about the truth. He considered strict adherence to it a sign of weakness, like being afraid of mice. He said whatever came into his head; he then believed it himself and tried to make everyone else believe it.

At the time I didn't know that all Mike's friends had to be "wealty" or "prrrominent." People who weren't his friends were "damn appleknockers."

I invited Mike to our house to meet the family and we spent a delightful evening listening to Mother and Mike reminisce about the fabulous days in Butte when copper mining was at its peak.

Mike's home and prosperous lumber business were located in a small town in the heart of the apple country in eastern Washington. September is the peak of the apple harvest, and September that year marked the entrance into the lives of my family of an endless procession of Railway Express trucks bearing gifts from Mike. The first truck brought 24 boxes of apples. Each apple was about six inches in diameter. We learned that Mike always bought not only the most but the biggest. From that day on for years our house smelled like a cider press and buzzed like a beehive with children dashing down to the basement for apples.

That first load of apples established Mike in the hearts of my daughters, Anne and Joan, who were five and six. There were many times later on when Mike irritated me, but not once did the children's adoration of him waver. No wonder; his "the most and biggest" slogan was the answer to every child's dream.

"I just love grapes," Anne mentioned to Mike one day. The next week the expressman delivered two 25-pound lugs of them. "Cherries are my favorite fruit," said Joan, so every week every year in cherry season Mike sent ten-pound boxes of enormous hand-packed cherries.

From Mike's friends we learned that his gifts were the only things they dreaded about him. If someone mentioned that he liked a certain kind of potato, next day Mike would have a ton of some other kind dumped in his front yard. Someone else would admit to a taste for a variety of ham, and would immediatley receive ten of a kind that Mike fancied. Someone else would show Mike a Cape Cod lighter he had bought, and Mike would get 90 and distribute them by the half dozen, even to people who had no fireplaces. And Mike was like a child with his gifts—demanding that you like what he brought and forcing you to open, while he stood by beaming, a box containing 144 jars of Indian chutney.

I surmise that Mike's obsession for wealth and prominence was an effort to obliterate a humble beginning, but I'm not sure, for neither I nor any of his many friends ever had the slightest idea what his background had been. Once he told me that his father had been a British sea captain and his mother a Russian. Then all of Mike's wealty prrrominent friends began shouting about communism, and Mike dropped that story like a hot rock. When I reminded him of it he denied ever having said it.

"My mudder was Swedish," he said. "My fadder died when I was a baby so I don't know what he was."

Mike drove a car as he did everything else, in superlatives— the worst and the fastest. Fortunately his car was bright red and when people saw him coming they could pull off into the brush until the comet had gone by. His method of driving was to climb behind the wheel, jam the accelerator clear to the floor, and call everyone who got in his way a damn apple-knocker.

Two weeks before the first Christmas after we met, Mike dropped in to find out what gifts my children wanted. He said, "I know Santa Claus very well." Joan said, "Of course—you're old enough!" Mike laughed delightedly and got out his notebook and pen. Anne said that she wanted a baby doll, a doll buggy, a toy sewing machine and "ball berrian" roller skates. Joan said that she wanted a bicycle, an electric train, a BB gun and "ball berrian" roller skates.

I said, "I also know Santa Claus, and he happens to be working for the government this year at a very bum salary and you'd better cut down those lists right now before he notices what little pigs you are." The children gave me dirty looks and changed their lists to a doll, train, paintboxes and ball-bearing roller skates.

Three days before Christmas the Railway Express delivered to our house what seemed to be the entire toy section of the Sears, Roebuck catalogue. On Christmas morning Anne and Joan were completely overcome. Mike had proved he knew Santa Claus.

Mike's entertaining was in perfect character—the biggest and most. He lived in an apartment located under his lumber-mill offices, and furnished in a style recognizable to my family as pure Butte. Everything in Mike's apartment was red, everything was monogrammed, and the place was heated to 80 degrees. In his bathroom were red velvet draperies with huge gold monograms, scented toilet paper, monogrammed soap, an Oriental rug, and a shelf full of bottles of expensive perfumes. The other rooms, also magnificently overdressed, contained such unusual bric-a-brac as a lamp composed of a semi-nude harem beauty gazing into a lighted crystal ball. Mike's chinaware was Tower-pattern Spode, which he called "Spud."

A delightful host, he knew the formula for a successful party: good food, good wine and congenial people. Any occasion was the signal for a party at Mike's, and people drove hundreds of miles over the mountains to attend. He drank very little himself but often mixed for his guests concoctions that would roll back the scalp. At one of his parties he had fruits and flowers frozen into each corner of a 200-pound block of ice, the center of which was hollowed out to form a punch bowl.

Mike was a superb cook and had trained his Filipino boy to be a gourmet's delight, but his meals were so enormous they made eating seem futile. I remember one picnic he gave. The eight of us in my family were instructed by Mike to be at the appointed place on the Skykomish River at two o'clock; we were to bring nothing but ourselves. When we got there Mike had already arrived; he had unloaded and spread under the trees 25 pounds of fried chicken; ten pounds of hamburgers made of beef tenderloin; ten pounds of weenies; eight cases of pop and beer; a vat of potato salad; pickles, olives, hard-boiled eggs; and a gallon of cocktails. Mike, who never ate during the day, didn't eat a mouthful; but he complained bitterly because we didn't completely demolish those mountains of food.

The one trait of Mike's which I found almost unbearable was the one which endeared him the most to the children. This was his bossiness and the "prrrogrrrams" he imposed on his guests. When Mike planned a party or a trip he planned it down to the last split second and his guests did what he wanted them to, when he wanted them to, or else!

When we went to visit him by train he would meet us at the station and hustle us to the car, outlining "de prrrogrrram" as we went. "De first stop," he would say, "is for lunch. Don't eat much. I am giving a dinner tonight and I want you to save your appetites. After lunch we visit Margaret, den Corinne, den Berle, den Marguerite, den Bea, den Doctor's wife, den home to rest up for dinner. I'm having ten couples but I've told dem dey can't stay late because we have to get an early start in de morning to drive to Lake Chelan. We'll stop dere for a minute while you look at de view, den on to Coulee Dam, about ten minutes will cover dat, den on to Moses Lake."

He was true to his word, too. It makes me tired and mad just to write about it, but the children loved it. Quick changes of scene and always on the go made their visits to Mike's perfect.

Another thing they loved about those visits was the fact that Mike got up at four, and when they came pattering down at five, instead of being batted back to bed as was the habit at home, they were greeted cordially and given coffee and leftover desserts for breakfast.

Children were the true love of Mike's life and he always treated them with dignity and courtesy. No matter how busy he was, he would listen gravely to stories of crabby teachers, unfair mothers, cheating playmates, interesting dreams and exciting movies. Mike had no sense of humor according to my standards, but no child's joke was ever too shopworn or obvious to go unapplauded.

Mike had a stock phrase for anything he liked: "Beautiful, beautiful, beautiful!" He applied it to the singing of John Charles Thomas (whom Mike admired tremendously and called John Charlie Thompson), autumn leaves, a plate of fudge, a child's new shoes, a load of lumber. As long as we live, members of our family will, when we see autumn leaves, echo Mike's "Beautiful, beautiful, beautiful, just like gold!"

When I married Donald MacDonald in 1942, after being courted by Mike via the Railway Express for eight years, I thought with relief that at last the deluge of presents would stop. It didn't. Mike and Don met, and the admiration was mutual. Don thought Mike was amazing, amusing and very dear. Mike referred to Don as "a great big handsome fellow—a Scotchman just like me." The presents continued but took a new form. Little motors, 50 gallons of antifreeze and cases of Scotch replaced the nylons and soap. The fruit continued. Mike was courting us both.

During the years I knew him, I tried to think of things to do for Mike, of ways to repay his generosity. I made him sketches, I sent him pictures, I was always on the lookout for something I could afford that he didn't already have 60 of. Then Don and I together took up the cause, but it was a losing game: every time we sent Mike a present he sent one back that was twice as big and eight times as expensive.

It was a problem that loomed bigger with the years until in 1945 I wrote a book called *The Egg and I* and suddenly became, to my surprise, both "wealty and prrrominent." I couldn't have done anything that would have repaid Mike more fully. He carried dozens of copies of the book in his car and tossed them at people with: "Sold ten million copies—now on the 86th printing. Biggest thing since the Bible."

When Mike died in 1948, his many friends outdid themselves in giving him a lavish funeral. Usually I avoid funerals, considering them outmoded and barbaric rites, but this one was just what Mike would have wanted. The altar and even the walls of the church were blanketed in flowers, and the coffin was entirely covered with orchids. "Beautiful, beautiful, beautiful!" he would have said.

The minister gave a short eulogy on Mike, his kindness and

generosity, his love of children, and ended with the assurance that the deceased had entered the kingdom of heaven. I hoped the minister was wrong, for I knew that Mike would much prefer to be with all the "wealty prrrominent" people.

The Extraordinary Helen Keller: A Portrait At 70

by Ishbel Ross

Helen Keller, at 70, has an ageless quality about her—inherent even in her looks—in keeping with her amazing life story. Blind, deaf and mute from early childhood, she rose above her triple handicap to become one of the best-known characters in the modern world, and is today (in 1950) an inspiration to both the blind and the seeing everywhere.

Although warmed by the universal interest in her, she has no wish to be set aside from the rest of mankind. She believes the blind should live and work like their fellows, unremarked and with full responsibility. In the inner quiet of her own dark castle she builds up strength and force to spend on her fellow afficted. Each decade brings her fresh wisdom, and some accentuation of her highly developed powers.

Those closest to her observe that her articulation improved noticeably in her 60's. She frequently makes recordings, and the voice of Helen Keller—which in itself represents one of the chief areas of effort in her life—is heard across the world. Her mastery of speech has been called "the greatest individual achievement in the history of education."

Helen, at ten years old, already was reading Braille avidly and could communicate by means of the manual alphabet. That spring of 1890 she learned of a deaf, dumb and blind Norwegian girl who had been taught to talk. Helen burned with ambition. Like lightning she spelled into Anne Sullivan's hand: "I must speak."

Miss Sullivan took Helen to Miss Sarah Fuller, principal of the Horace Mann School for the Deaf in Boston. Miss Fuller went to work at once, passing Helen's hand lightly over the lower part of her face, and putting Helen's fingers into her mouth, so that she might feel the position of the teacher's tongue, her teeth, the movement of the lower jaw and the course of the trachea.

Miss Fuller then set her tongue in the bed of the jaw just behind the lower front teeth for the sound of *i* in *it*. Next she put Helen's forefinger against her teeth, another finger on her throat and repeated the sound *ĭ* several times. As soon as she had ceased, Helen's "fingers flew to her own mouth and throat and, after arranging her tongue and teeth, she uttered a sound so nearly like what I had made that it seemed an echo of it."

Then they practiced the vowels *a* and *o*, which Helen repeated distinctly. After this they tried the words *mama* and *papa*. Miss Fuller delicately pronounced the word *mama*, at the same time drawing her finger along the back length of Helen's hand to indicate the relative length of the two syllables. After a few repetitions, *mama* and *papa* came correctly and with "almost musical sweetness from her lips."

Going home in the streetcar after her seventh lesson, Helen turned to Miss Sullivan and said in "hollow, breathy tones": *I am not dumb now.* This was her first real use of words in conveying a thought, and it came within a month after her first lesson in articulation. It was human speech from the lips of one who, except for her early baby babblings, had reached the age of ten uttering only the uncouth sounds of the mute.

"We have a lesson to learn from this child," Dr. Alexander Graham Bell said. His own skepticism had been washed away earlier when he paid Helen an unexpected visit after receiving a letter from her so beautifully written and well composed that he could not believe the deaf, dumb and blind child was its author. However, he found her alone in a room, writing to someone else with equal skill and fluency. He became her close friend, and remained so to the end of his life.

Helen took 11 lessons from Miss Fuller, but this was only the beginning of her long tussle with speech. Week after week, month after month, year after year, she labored to improve enunciation. She repeated words and sentences for hours, using her fingers to catch the vibrations of Miss Sullivan's throat, the movement of her tongue and lips, the expression of her face as she talked.

She has never ceased to labor over her voice, to make speeches in public and to conduct much of her conversation by direct speech. Her voice has a keening quality, strange to listen to; her sentences are unaccented. She appears to speak with effort. Her clenched right hand describes a parabola and comes down briskly on her left palm, putting an emphatic period to her last sentence. At the same time her face relaxes in a most winning smile, erasing all impression of the great effort she seems to have made.

"I have only partially conquered the hostile silence," she says. "My voice is not a pleasant one. I am afraid, but I have clothed its broken wings in the unfailing hues of my dreams and my struggle for it has strengthened every fiber of my being and deepened my understanding of all human strivings and disappointed ambitions."

She became adept at reading lips by vibration. By placing the middle finger on the nose, her forefinger on the lips and her thumb on the larynx, she can "hear what others say," particularly if their speech is clear and resonant.

She found Franklin D. Roosevelt an ideal subject in this respect. She caught Mark Twain's best jokes by vibration. With her fingers on his lips Enrico Caruso "poured his golden voice" into her hand. Feodor Chaliapin shouted the "Volga Boat Song" with his arm encircling her tightly so that she could feel every vibration of his mighty voice. Jascha Heifetz played for her while her fingers rested lightly on his violin. She has read Carl Sandburg's verses from his lips and old plantation folk songs from the rim of his banjo. With her hand resting on a piano she detects "tiny quavers, returns of melody and the rush that follows." She gets some small response by vibration from radio, too.

The initial penetration of the dark mists that enshrouded Helen Keller dates back to 1886, when she was six years old. Born in the little Alabama town of Tuscumbia, she was a normal baby up to 19 months and seemed to enjoy the flowers, the flitting birds, the play of light and shadow. Then she was stricken with a "fever of brain and stomach." She was desperately ill, but the fever subsided almost as suddenly as it had begun.

Soon her mother noticed that Helen's eyes did not close when she bathed the child. She took her to an oculist and learned that Helen was blind. Next she noticed that the child did not respond to the loud ringing of a bell. Helen was deaf, too. Inevitably, by the age of three she was also mute, and such words as she had babbled at 18 months were forgotten.

Helen grew fast and was physically strong and well formed, but her good nature dissolved in frantic tantrums. Her failure to make herself understood was followed by wild gusts of rage. She would fling herself on the grass and give way to uncontrollable fits of screaming. Her table manners were appalling. She would not wash her face or button her shoes. Years later she wrote: "I felt as if invisible hands were holding me. I made frantic efforts to free myself."

Her gentle mother, cowed by such violence, gave in to her at every point. There was great power in Helen, instead of the apathy that usually rests heavily on the triply handicapped child. Here lay the germ of her future success. But, Mrs. Keller was close to despair when she picked up Charles Dickens' *American Notes* and read of Laura Bridgman, the deaf, mute and blind girl in New England whose mind had been reached by Samuel Gridley Howe.

Finally Helen was taken to Michael Anagnos, who had succeeded Dr. Howe as head of the Perkins Institution. He recommended as tutor an Irish girl who had just been graduated. This was Anne Sullivan, who was to be Helen Keller's inseparable companion for the next half century.

She was the child of Irish immigrants and her own childhood had a Dickensian touch. Her drunken father beat her. She was starved, bruised, neglected, and finally was abandoned to the almshouse as a state charge. She entered Perkins in 1880, blind from trachoma. Two operations virtually restored her sight, although she had trouble with her eyes all her life and became blind again in her later years.

Anne Sullivan, arriving in Alabama, was struck by Helen Keller's fine bearing and intelligent face, notwithstanding the fact that it "lacked mobility or soul." Helen rushed at her as she stepped down from the carriage, felt her dress and face, repulsed a caress, tried to open Miss Sullivan's bag and staged a scene on the doorstep when Mrs. Keller attempted to take it from her. Miss Sullivan produced a doll sent by the Perkins children. When Helen, quickly beguiled, had played with it for some time Miss Sullivan spelled into her hand the letters *d-o-l-l*. The child's attention was arrested by this unfamiliar maneuver and she tried to imitate the finger motions. This was the first conscious effort ever made to teach Helen Keller.

When Miss Sullivan took away the doll a tussle began. It was the first of many. The new teacher moved Helen away from her distracted parents to an adjoining cottage. A herculean battle of wills raged for several days. It was a physical as well as a mental struggle, but Miss Sullivan won, even though she had to hold Helen down by force for two hours at a time to quell her fierce resistance. "Her restless spirit gropes in the dark," Teacher commented. "Her untaught, unsatisfied hands destroy whatever they touch because they do not know what else to do with things."

She noticed that the child already had sundry ways of indicating her wishes. If she longed for ice cream she turned the handle of an imaginary freezer. For bread and butter she went through the motions of cutting and spreading. She pretended to put on glasses to symbolize her father. She took to rocking the new doll, making a monotonous chanting sound with her lips and touching them lightly with her fingers. But she also learned to spell new words by the manual language—pin, hat, cup and verbs like sit, stand and walk.

Within two weeks a gleam of light dawned. Miss Sullivan took her to the pump house and drew water. As it flowed into the mug and over the child's right hand she spelled *w-a-t-e-r* into the other.

"The word, coming so close upon the sensation of cold

water rushing over her hand, seemed to startle her," Miss Sullivan wrote. "She dropped the mug and stood as one transfixed. A new light came into her face."

Helen's own recollection is: "Somehow the mystery of language was revealed to me. I knew then that water meant the wonderful cool something that flowed over my hand. That living word awakened my soul; gave it light, hope, joy; set it free!"

Helen returned to the house in a fever of excitement, touching everything as she moved, visibly seeking its name. The ground, the trellis, the bushes, the pump—she knew now that everything had a name and she wished to know what it was. Within the space of a few hours she had added 30 new words to her vocabulary. From that point on her education proceeded with uncanny speed. "The eagerness with which she absorbs ideas is delightful," Miss Sullivan related. "It is a rare privilege to watch the birth, growth and first feeble struggles of a living mind."

Miss Sullivan taught her to read with little sentences slipped into a frame, after each separate word—raised on cardboard—had been placed beside its object, like *doll is on bed*.

"When her fingers light on words she knows," Miss Sillivan wrote, "she fairly screams with pleasure and hugs and kisses me for joy. When I gave her my Braille slate to amuse her the little witch soon was writing letters. I had no idea she knew what a letter was."

At the end of three months Helen knew 400 words and many idioms. That summer the game went on for hours at a time, outdoors and in. They studied under tulip and mulberry trees, and everything that could "hum or buzz or sing or bloom" was part of Helen's education. She felt the downy peaches in the orchard, squeezed the bursting cotton bolls, caught an insect in a plucked flower. She learned to distinguish mountain laurel from honeysuckle, and a pig from a hen. Miss Sullivan made raised maps in clay for her pupil, with strings and orange sticks for equator, meridians and poles. She taught Helen to count by stringing beads in groups, and arranging kindergarten straws for addition and subtraction. It was the only subject the child disliked. Her pencil writing soon was excellent. Within a month after trying it, she wrote a correctly spelled and legible letter to her cousin. Miss Keller's handwriting was square, artistic and always legible.

By the end of August she knew 625 words. But after a year's instruction Helen had become extremely pale and thin. Everyone thought her overtaxed and driven. This charge was to be made later when Helen was preparing for Radcliffe, but the teacher's immediate comment was: "So far nobody seems to have thought of chloroforming her, which is, I think, the only effective way of stopping the natural exercise of her faculties."

At this point Helen became quite fond of dress and finery and insisted on having her hair put up in curls, no matter how exhausting her day had been.

Miss Sullivan took Helen to Perkins Institution when she was eight, and a whole new world opened up for her. She had Braille books to read and she could associate with other children who knew the manual alphabet. She soon displayed sensational abilities. Miss Sullivan let her browse from book to book, picking out words at random, long before she could actually read them. She worked on a systematic basis, studying arithmetic, geography, zoology, botany and reading. This was no longer the free and spontaneous education of the outdoors, but Helen toiled over every aspect of her work, refusing to leave a task unfinished. When urged to rest she would say: "It will give me strength if I finish it *now*." This habit of tireless industry persisted, even in her 70's.

These were days of great mental growth for Helen. As she and her teacher traveled, Teacher spelled into her hand fluent descriptions of the passing scene—the hills and rivers, the hamlets and cities, the way people looked and what they wore. They summered on Cape Cod and Helen learned to swim, but her first splash into the sea brought a great surprise. No one had thought to tell her that there was salt in the ocean! She learned to row and sail, to ride and use a tandem bicycle.

The intellectuals of Boston were taking stock of this brilliant girl. Oliver Wendell Holmes wept when she recited Tennyson's "Break, break, break" to him in halting sentences. John Greenleaf Whittier told her he could understand every word she said, which made Helen happy. She corresponded with famous men, writing to them both in French and English. By this time she was tall, graceful, and showed charm and humor.

College was the next step. Helen settled on Radcliffe and prepared with her usual thoroughness. She entered the Gilman

School for Young Ladies in Cambridge and was intensively tutored, with Miss Sullivan always by her side to read the lectures into her hand. In 1900 she enrolled at Radcliffe, the first individual with a triple handicap to enter an institution of higher learning.

But college was a disappointment to Helen. She did well, but felt the lack of time for meditation. She could not take notes during lectures because her hands were "busy listening." She jotted down what she could remember when she got home. She used a Braille writer for algebra, geometry and physics, but she had little aptitude for mathematics. Examinations were a nightmare. But she enjoyed some of her classes and she and Teacher worked with their usual wholehearted concentration. They got Brailled books from Germany and England, and Helen read until her fingers bled.

Helen was graduated in 1904, taking special honors in English. She was 24 years old. Already requests were flowing in for appearances and for magazine articles. She was invited to the St. Louis Exposition in 1904 to awaken world-wide interest in the education of the deaf-blind. But on Helen Keller Day the crowds got out of hand. Her dress was torn to shreds. The roses were snatched from her hat.

She prepared to lecture by taking special lessons with a music teacher. Again she strove for a regulated pitch. At times her voice would become unmanageable. It would dive down or go soaring up beyond her control. Rain, wind, dust or excitement affected its pitch. But in 1913 she made her first public-speaking appearance.

"My mind froze," Helen commented at the time. She prayed. Words rose to her lips, but she could not utter a syllable. At last she forced out a sound that felt to her like a cannon going off. Later she was told it was only a whisper.

But after this Miss Keller and Teacher made many appearances in public. Teacher would demonstrate how she had taught young Helen. The pupil then would speak, winding up with the phrase: *I am not dumb now*. In 1914 they set out on the first of a number of transcontinental speaking tours. By this time a brisk and capable young Scottish girl, Polly Thomson, had joined them as secretary and manager. They went to Hollywood to make the film *Deliverance*. Then they embarked on a dignified vaudeville act, Miss Keller causing a sensation at the Palace in New York. Helen loved it. She found vaudeville full of life, color and variety. She "felt the breath of the audience in her face."

. Helen Keller was known now around the world. Her books were translated into many languages, as well as into Braille. In the 1930s she began her international traveling. She went repeatedly to Europe, then to the Orient, interested always in the blind, talking for the blind, raising money for the blind. Those who had read about her now turned out to see her. By this time she was learned, composed and equal to any emergency. She received honorary degrees and decorations in many lands.

But Teacher's health was failing. She was almost blind. No longer could she keep up with the vigorous and healthy Helen. She died in 1936, shortly after the last of a long series of eye operations. That year the Roosevelt medal for "Coöperative Achievement of Unique Character and Far-Reaching Significance" was awarded to this remarkable pair.

Today—in 1950—Miss Keller and Miss Thomson live in a graceful rambling house set in the Connecticut woods near Westport. A stone Japanese lantern, eight feet high, stands symbolically in one corner of the lawn with a constantly burning light—not to go out while Helen Keller lives. A winding path leads from her garden to the woods, and here she likes to stroll and meditate alone, except for her dogs, moving along with her hand lightly touching a rustic handrail.

Miss Keller spends long hours sitting tall and straight at the typewriter in her study, writing, or filling requests for messages. Around the walls are her Braille books, which she reads until the fingertips that have traveled over so many miles of Braille have to be bound with silk for protection. She reads in the dark or the daylight, like all the blind, who sleep poorly and do not know night from day. Miss Thomson reads her the day's headlines at breakfast and she chooses the news stories she wishes to hear. Articles that closely touch her interests are sometimes Brailled for her.

Miss Keller can smell the woods and flowers beyond her windows. She knows when it rains or snows, when the sun shines or the day is gray, when the early grass comes up, the roses bloom, the leaves wither and smoke trails from autumn bonfires. She has her own suite shut off from the rest of the house and there she functions in complete independence. Everything is kept in perfect order. She tidies her own bathroom, makes her own bed, keeps her papers in place, emerges neat as a pin in the morning, often as early as five o'clock. She and Miss Thomson garden at dawn, when the weather is right. She likes to cut grass, to weed and to rake leaves.

She looks extraordinarily young for 70, her face unlined, her hair only lightly streaked with gray. Her eyes are blue and bright; not the lackluster eyes of the blind, but alive and expressive.

Helen Keller is deeply spiritual and knows great stretches of her Brailled Bible by heart. Her faith sustains her in the quiet hours when she retreats from her busy life into the deep silence that only the deaf, blind and mute can know. Around her shines the steady flame of character, purpose and hard work.

"I look forward to the world to come," she says, "where all physical limitations will drop from me like shackles; where I shall again find my beloved Teacher, and engage joyously in greater service than I have yet known."

IN JUNE 1968 THE LIGHT WAS EXTINGUISHED. HELEN KELLER HAD DIED, SHORTLY BEFORE HER 88TH BIRTHDAY.

Diamond Jim
by Parker Morell

The scene is a lobster palace of the 1890s. Centered in the room, a table, staggering under a profusion of viands; at the table, nine women and one grandiose man, two large steaks before him. He weighs over 240 pounds; eyes small and shrewd; the jaw is a jowl. Tied around his neck is an oversize napkin. If on his knee, it would have been lost beneath New York's best known stomach—a stomach starting impetuously at the neck and curving majestically down. But every eye is held, not by these things, but by the dozens of diamonds, glittering winks of light, enormous like the person. Diamond Jim Brady! Solomon in all his glory....

One evening in 1856, Daniel Brady swung into his West Street saloon, shouting, "It's a boy! 'Tis me the drinks are on this night!" And throughout the life of Jim, whose health was then drunk, it was always: "Drinks by courtesy of Brady." Diamond Jim himself never drank, but his stock in trade was in making friends with convivial men. When he was 11, Jim thumbed his nose at the saloon and became a bellboy; at 15, he was joyously slinging trunks around Grand Central baggage room; at 23, he went on the road, selling railroad supplies. He proved the most successful salesman his firm ever employed.

"If you're goin' to make money, you gotta look like money." So Jim lavished care like a bride's upon his going-away outfit— Prince Albert, stovepipe hat—but the most important item, his first diamond ring! Immediately, the Brady luck began to show. The next decade offered the greatest market for railroad supplies in history; Jim used to say that his hardest job was writing out his orders. Commissions piled up, and so did his collection of diamonds. They made money for him.

"Speaking of diamonds, you might like to see these. They're my hobby." And before the railroad official's eyes he would spread out a handful. If a tough customer exclaimed, "they're imitations," Jim would stride to a window and write "James Buchanan Brady" on the pane. His point was won—more important, his name was there to be remembered.

Jim's fame spread over the entire railroad system, and the inevitable "Diamond Jim" became the most valuable nickname in America. His prosperity grew with the years. Still selling supplies, he became vice-president of the Standard Steel Car Company, just when steel cars were selling at a breakneck pace. Finally Jim realized, "Hell, I'm rich! It's time I had some fun!"

He entered a new world, made for Jim and he for it. Vulgar, blatant, garish, it put both hands into Jim's wallet, and Jim smiled happily. He became a chronic first-nighter, always in a front-row seat; at fashionable Manhattan Beach he was one of the larger landmarks; he was among the Wall Street potentates at the Waldorf bar. Drinking only milk or orange juice, he was said to open more wine than anyone in New York. With his infallible flair for headliners, he fraternized with John L. Sullivan, Stanford White, Augustin Daly and Lillian Russell, whose beauty was enthralling New York, Asking only to bask in her smile, he was her close friend for 40 years. During the "Bicycle Cycle," when the world was awheel, Jim bought for her a machine that evoked awe. It was gold-plated and studded with chip diamonds; handlebars of mother-of-pearl; spokes twinkling with diamonds and rubies.

But Jim's real moment came when the newspapers announced: "JAMES B. BRADY DRIVES FIRST HORSELESS CARRIAGE IN CITY. TRAFFIC TIED UP TWO HOURS." He had provided a sensation for the town.

In the 1900s, people thought nothing of tackling a 14-course dinner. They *were* moved to wonder, however, when they saw Diamond Jim breaking bread. Not only did he eat Gargantuan meals, but he put away three and four helpings of the main dishes. Then, to make the food "set better," he ate a box of chocolates. Incidentally, most of Jim's parties were charged to his now unlimited expense accounts. He had early discovered that more wares could be sold at 3 a.m. than in broad daylight. His closest friends could never determine where Jim's business left off and pleasure began. It was a new technique in salesmanship.

For more entertaining Jim bought a country place—"nothing elaborate, just for weekends." But America and Europe were scoured for what the well-dressed farmhouse would wear. One story said that Jim's cows were milked into diamond-studded buckets of solid gold. This was untrue—the buckets were only plated. From this farm he shipped each week 35 huge zinc hampers, packed with delicacies, to actors, to railroad clerks or starving chorus girls—anyone whose poverty Jim knew. Year in, year out he played the good provider. An office clerk was kept busy with weekly gifts to more than 300 recipients—fruit, flowers, stockings, or candy (Jim's sweetmeat bills ran $2000 a month).

To climax his orgy of spending, Jim was inspired to own a different set of jewelry for every day of the month; for a starter, the Transportation Set. It featured every animal or appliance concerned in carrying men or goods; an engine-wheel ring, with a 10-carat center and 42 smaller diamonds; a camel, a donkey, an automobile. Completed, the set held 2548 stones. The other sets followed rapidly, each of 14 items, from studs to underwear buttons, and with its own watch. To Jim it was beautiful. "You fellers talk about what's done and what ain't, but I notice that them as has 'em wears 'em!"

Inevitably, Jim's princely habits attracted the predatory. "One night," said George Rector, "more than a dozen people came over to Jim's table to borrow money, and every time Jim brought out a handful of bills. Finally I said, 'Mr. Brady, aren't you letting people take advantage of you?' He closed one eye in a wink: 'George, I know they're pulling my leg. But it's fun to be a sucker—if you can afford it.'"

One night in 1912, Diamond Jim lay in his great mahogany bed waiting to be rushed to Johns Hopkins Hospital for a desperate operation—a million-to-one chance. Roaring at others to leave the room, Jim sent his secretary for certain papers from his safe. "There's $200,000 in personal notes here. They can't pay. Burn 'em." "But—" the secretary was aghast. "Burn the whole lot! If I'm gonna die, I'm gonna die. But I ain't gonna leave troubles behind me. Burn 'em." This was Jim's legacy to Broadway.

At the hospital, Jim caused a sensation: the fluoroscope showed his stomach *six times the normal size*. Directly after the operation, the surgeon, Dr. Young, was obliged to sail for a conference abroad. "On reaching the boat," he said later, "I found my modest stateroom changed for the boat's most luxurious suite—flowers, fruit, champagne—all planned by Mr. Brady, whom the doctors had given 24 hours to live. He could think of such things while on what he considered his deathbed."

During convalescence, Jim reveled in attentions. The nurses couldn't believe that all this jewelry (he bedecked himself in a different set each day) was real. He secretly ordered 50 two-carat rings; then, one by one he called in the nurses: "Here, if the pawnbroker tells you this is real, you keep it." But when Dr. Young returned, Jim was not thinking of diamonds and pretty girls. "Say, Doctor, this urology business is kinda interesting, ain't it? Does all this experimentin' take a lot of money?" "It certainly does, Mr. Brady." "Y'know, I been thinkin' I'd kinda like to help a bit. I'm a rich man, and I ain't got a damn thing to do with my money. . . ." Three years later the doors of the Brady Urological Institute were opened.

To the last, life was great fun for Diamond Jim. He died in his sleep in his $1000-a-week quarters at Atlantic City. They buried him on April 16, 1917. While his body, decked out in his No. 1 Diamond Set, lay in his own house, the police had to handle the crowds paying their last respects. The entire first floor was filled with flowers, from thousand-dollar orchid blankets to ten-cent nosegays timidly laid at his coffin by newsboys whom he had befriended. Except for bequests to close friends, all his money went to charity—hospitals, newsboys' lodging houses, an orphan asylum, the Children's Aid Society. Diamond Jim had realized the truth: "It is more blessed to give . . ." But he would have expressed it: "Hell, what's money to me! I gotta have some fun!"

My Friend, Albert Einstein

by Banesh Hoffmann

He was one of the greatest scientists the world has ever known, yet if I had to convey the essence of Albert Einstein in a single word, I would choose *simplicity*. Perhaps an anecdote will help. Once, caught in a downpour, he took off his hat and held it under his coat. Asked why, he explained, with admirable logic, that the rain would damage the hat, but his hair would be none the worse for its wetting. This knack for going instinctively to the heart of a matter was the secret of his major scientific discoveries—this and his extraordinary feeling for beauty.

I first met Albert Einstein in 1935, at the famous Institute for Advanced Study in Princeton, N.J. He had been among the first to be invited to the Institute, and was offered *carte blanche* as to salary. To the director's dismay, Einstein asked for an impossible sum: it was far too *small*. The director had to plead with him to accept a larger salary.

I was in awe of Einstein, and hesitated before approaching him about some ideas I had been working on. When I finally knocked on his door, a gentle voice said, "Come"—with a rising inflection that made the single word both a welcome and a question. I entered his office and found him seated at a table, calculating and smoking his pipe. Dressed in ill-fitting clothes, his hair characteristically awry, he smiled a warm welcome. His utter naturalness at once set me at ease.

As I began to explain my ideas, he asked me to write the equations on the blackboard so he could see how they developed. Then came the staggering—and altogether endearing—request: "Please go slowly. I do not understand things quickly." This from Einstein! He said it gently, and I laughed. From then on, all vestiges of fear were gone.

Burst of Genius. Einstein was born in 1879 in the German city of Ulm. He had been no infant prodigy; indeed, he was so late in learning to speak that his parents feared he was a dullard. In school, though his teachers saw no special talent in him, the signs were already there. He taught himself calculus, for example, and his teachers seemed a little afraid of him because he asked questions they could not answer. At the age of 16, he asked himself whether a light wave would seem stationary if one ran abreast of it. From that innocent question would arise, ten years later, his theory of relativity.

Einstein failed his entrance examinations at the Swiss Federal Polytechnic School, in Zurich, but was admitted a year later. There he went beyond his regular work to study the masterworks of physics on his own. Rejected when he applied for academic positions, he ultimately found work, in 1902, as a patent examiner in Berne, and there in 1905 his genius burst into fabulous flower.

Among the extraordinary things he produced in that memorable year were his theory of relativity, with its famous offshoot, $E = mc^2$ (energy equals mass times the speed of light squared), and his quantum theory of light. These two theories were not only revolutionary, but seemingly contradictory: the former was intimately linked to the theory that light consists of waves, while the latter said it consists somehow of particles. Yet this unknown young man boldly proposed both at once—

and he was right in both cases, though how he could have been is far too complex a story to tell here.

Mental Magic. Collaborating with Einstein was an unforgettable experience. In 1937, the Polish physicist Leopold Infeld and I asked if we could work with him. He was pleased with the proposal, since he had an idea about gravitation waiting to be worked out in detail. Thus we got to know not merely the man and the friend, but also the professional.

The intensity and depth of his concentration were fantastic. When battling a recalcitrant problem, he worried it as an animal worries its prey. Often, when we found ourselves up against a seemingly insuperable difficulty, he would stand up, put his pipe on the table, and say in his quaint English, "I will a little tink" (he could not pronounce "th"). Then he would pace up and down, twirling a lock of his long, graying hair around his forefinger.

A dreamy, faraway and yet inward look would come over his face. There was no appearance of concentration, no furrowing of the brow—only a placid inner communion. The minutes would pass, and then suddenly Einstein would stop pacing as his face relaxed into a gentle smile. He had found the solution to the problem. Sometimes it was so simple that Infeld and I could have kicked ourselves for not having thought of it. But the magic had been performed invisibly in the depths of Einstein's mind, by a process we could not fathom.

When his wife died he was deeply shaken, but insisted that now more than ever was the time to be working hard. I remember going to his house to work with him during that sad time. His face was haggard and grief-lined, but he put forth a great effort to concentrate. To help him, I steered the discussion away from routine matters into more difficult theoretical problems, and Einstein gradually became absorbed in the discussion. We kept at it for some two hours, and at the end his eyes were no longer sad. As I left, he thanked me with moving sincerity. "It was a fun," he said. He had had a moment of surcease from grief, and then groping words expressed a deep emotion.

Ideas From God. Although Einstein felt no need for religious ritual and belonged to no formal religious group, he was the most deeply religious man I have known. He once said to me, "Ideas come from God," and one could hear the capital "G" in the reverence with which he pronounced the word. On the marble fireplace in the mathematics building at Princeton University is carved, in the original German, what one might call his scientific credo: "God is subtle, but he is not malicious." By this Einstein meant that scientists could expect to find their task difficult, but not hopeless: the Universe was a Universe of law, and God was not confusing us with deliberate paradoxes and contradictions.

Einstein was an accomplished amateur musician. We used to play duets, he on the violin, I at the piano. One day he surprised me by saying Mozart was the greatest composer of all. Beethoven "created" his music, but the music of Mozart was of such purity and beauty one felt he had merely "found" it—that it had always existed as part of the inner beauty of the Universe, waiting to be revealed.

It was this very Mozartean simplicity that most characterized Einstein's methods. His 1905 theory of relativity, for example, was built on just two simple assumptions. One is the so-called principle of relativity, which means, roughly speaking, that we cannot tell whether we are at rest or moving smoothly. The other assumption is that the speed of light is the same no matter what the speed of the object that produces it. You can see how reasonable this is if you think of agitating a stick in a lake to create waves. Whether you wiggle the stick from a stationary pier, or from a rushing speedboat, the waves. once generated, are on their own, and their speed has nothing to do with that of the stick.

Each of these assumptions, by itself, was so plausible as to seem primitively obvious. But together they were in such violent conflict that a lesser man would have dropped one or the other and fled in panic. Einstein daringly kept both—and by so doing he revolutionized physics. For he demonstrated they could, after all, exist peacefully side by side, provided we gave up cherished beliefs about the nature of time.

Science is like a house of cards, with concepts like time and space at the lowest level. Tampering with time brought most of the house tumbling down, and it was this that made Einstein's work so important—and controversial. At a conference in Princeton in honor of his 70th birthday, one of the speakers, a Nobel Prize-winner, tried to convey the magical quality of Einstein's achievement. Words failed him, and with a shrug of helplessness he pointed to his wristwatch, and said in tones of awed amazement, "It all came from this." His very ineloquence made this the most eloquent tribute I have heard to Einstein's genius.

Sand Sense. Although fame had little effect on Einstein as a person, he could not escape it; he was, of course, instantly recognizable. One autumn Saturday, I was walking with him in Princeton discussing some technical matters. Parents and alumni were streaming excitedly toward the stadium, their minds on the coming football game. As they approached us, they paused in sudden recognition, and a momentary air of solemnity came over them as if they had been reminded of a different world. Yet Einstein seemed totally unaware of this effect and went on with the discussion as though they were not there.

We think of Einstein as one concerned only with the deepest aspects of science. But he saw scientific principles in everyday things to which most of us would give barely a second thought. He once asked me if I had ever wondered why a man's feet will sink into either dry or completely submerged sand, while sand that is merely damp provides a firm surface. When I could not answer, he offered a simple explanation.

It depends, he pointed out, on *surface tension*, the elastic-skin effect of a liquid surface. This is what holds a drop together, or causes two small raindrops on a windowpane to pull into one big drop the moment their surfaces touch.

When sand is damp, Einstein explained, there are tiny amounts of water between grains. The surface tensions of these tiny amounts of water pull all the grains together, and friction then makes them hard to budge. When the sand is dry, there is obviously no water between grains. If the sand is fully immersed, there is water between grains, but no water *surface* to pull them together.

This is not as important as relativity; yet there is not telling what seeming trifle will lead an Einstein to a major discovery. And the puzzle of the sand does give us an inkling of the power and elegance of his mind.

Cosmic Simplicity. Einstein's work, performed quietly with pencil and paper, seemed remote from the turmoil of everyday life: But his ideas were so revolutionary they caused violent controversy and irrational anger. Indeed, in order to be able to award him a belated Nobel Prize, the selection committee had to avoid mentioning relativity, and pretend the prize was awarded primarily for his work on the quantum theory.

Political events upset the serenity of his life even more. When the Nazis came to power in Germany, his theories were officially declared false because they had been formulated by a Jew. His property was confiscated, and it is said a price was put on his head.

When scientists in the United States, fearful that the Nazis might develop an atomic bomb, sought to alert American authorities to the danger, they were scarcely heeded. In desperation, they drafted a letter which Einstein signed and sent directly to President Roosevelt. It was this act that led to the fateful decision to go all-out on the production of an atomic bomb—an endeavor in which Einstein took no active part. When he heard of the agony and destruction that his $E = mc^2$ had wrought, he was dismayed beyond measure, and from then on there was a look of ineffable sadness in his eyes.

There was something elusively whimsical about Einstein. It is illustrated by my favorite anecdote about him. In his first year in Princeton, on Christmas Eve, so the story goes, some children sang carols outside his house. Having finished, they knocked on his door and explained they were collecting money to buy Christmas presents. Einstein listened, then said, "Wait a moment." He put on his scarf and overcoat, and took his violin from its case. Then, joining the children as they went from door to door, he accompanied their singing of "Silent Night" on his violin.

How shall I sum up what is meant to have known Einstein and his works? Like the Nobel Prize-winner who pointed helplessly at his watch, I can find no adequate words. It was akin to the revelation of great art that lets one see what was formerly hidden. And when, for example, I walk on the sand of a lonely beach, I am reminded of his ceaseless search for cosmic simplicity—and the scene takes on a deeper, sadder beauty.

‖On the Job

HAL BOYLE,
NEWSPAPER COLUMNIST
by Saul Pett

The press agent was apoplectic. "Whadya mean you dunno where Hal Boyle is? He's supposed to have lunch with Jimmy Stewart. Today! *Now!* A big Hollywood star comes all the way from the coast to be interviewed by Boyle, and you tell me you dunno where he is? I'll *kill* myself!"

Such traumatic scenes were part of the price one paid for working at a desk next to Harold Vincent Boyle, Associated Press columnist. It was a small expense for a large return.

Boyle could be maddening if you were married to him or employed him or worked next to him—or were merely waiting for him to keep an appointment. But you could never dislike him. Not his over-age, overweight, balding some kind of Huck Finn.

With a special grace, he wrote a human-interest column that endeared him to millions of readers of hundreds of papers. He was one of the two or three most widely read columnists in

America. He won a Pulitzer Prize and many other awards; his columns were read on radio and dramatized on TV, and reprinted in magazines. But his special effect was the devotion of his readers, who laughed and cried with him, and folded him up in their wallets or framed him on the wall.

While he wrote mostly from New York, his readers somehow felt he was just around the corner. "I began reading Hal Boyle as a boy in Danville, Va.," a reader once noted. "It was years before I discovered he didn't actually live in Danville."

That special kinship brought a forgiving Jimmy Stewart to New York for another crack at a Boyle interview. This time Hal managed to show up. The first time, it had slipped his mind as he fell into conversation with the boys coming off the night shift, and one thing had led to another. In fact, whatever conversation he was having at the moment tended to become uninterruptible. Or, as his wife, Frances, used to say, "Whoever gets to Hal first, wins."

He savored all occasions when men of goodwill forgathered to exchange pleasantries and profundities away from the tyranny of the typewriter. On one such occasion, the phone kept ringing at Pat Moriarty's bar, and Hal kept saying, "Pat, if that's Frances, tell her I just left."

Hours later, Hal reached home. He had missed a dinner party, and a baleful Frances Boyle began lecturing him sternly. But just then the phone happened to ring. "Frances," Hal sang out, "if that's Pat Moriarty, tell him I just left."

He could, even after hard nights, awake with more style than any other man I've known. Once, after a long evening of talk and drink aboard my boat, we went to sleep outside, in the cockpit. He awoke to find a large swan alongside, just a few inches from his nose. There they were, the long-necked, enigmatic swan and the short-necked, broken-nosed Irishman, eyeball to eyeball. "Damn it, stop worrying," said Boyle to the swan. "I'll get the column in on time."

Gentle Spirit. Hal Boyle used to come to work at the AP office in New York at 7 a.m. No amount of executive muscle could persuade him to clean up the pile of debris on his desk, which was said to conceal the first of the Dead Sea Scrolls and the last of Judge Crater. Insisting that "a neat desk is the sign of a frightened mind," Old Fearless refused to throw anything away. His hoard of old letters from readers, false column starts and ancient interview notes reached a height of two feet. Inexorably, the overflow slid onto the next desk—mine.

By 9 he was usually done with his column, and ready to start planning lunch. Somewhere between 3 and 5, he carefully considered the basics—who, what, when, where—of cocktails. A deceptively casual man, he did not take his pleasures lightly.

He did not take life lightly, either, but kept that fact largely hidden. He enjoyed his drink but that, by no means, was the be-all. People were his nourishment and he nourished them in return, both with his typewriter and with the pleasure of his company. A gentle spirit in an ungentle world, he was at peace with himself and his fellow man.

"I think this is a hard world," he said, "and I think every human in it, at one time or another, has a hard time. The thing I admire most is people who face life with courage, loyalty and a sense of humor."

He was a cornucopia of all three. But always, behind the rumpus room of the extrovert, always in a quiet, hidden room, there was the Boyle of the half-sung heart-song, the sweet sadness, the dreams that got away, the vague loneliness, the Boyle eternally aware that every man born of woman must die, that each day is both an arrival and a departure. There was Boyle, the head of the Walter Mitty lobby with a secret dream of telling somebody off just once, the Boyle who couldn't undertip a surly waiter or cut off an insistent bore despite internal bleeding, the gentle wit who kept the foil turned on himself, the loving chronicler of the faceless, the frustrated, the boy in every man.

A General's Thanks. He was born in 1911, the son of a Kansas City butcher, and grew up in a family of seven. He began as a copy boy in the AP Kansas City bureau, departed long enough to earn degrees in journalism and English at the University of Missouri, returned to AP as a reporter, and took off as a war correspondent with the invasion of North Africa in 1942.

He covered three wars in all—World War II, Korea and Vietnam—and as the loving Boswell of the GI won his Pulitzer in 1945. He was also particularly proud of the award given him by the Veterans of Foreign Wars for his coverage of Korea, because it was presented by his favorite officer, General of the Army Omar Bradley. "There are few men," Bradley said, "who understand the American soldier and how he feels as well as you."

Boyle would have been pleased—so mightily pleased it would have shushed him into embarrassed silence—to know that at the end, when all wars were over for him, there was a huge wreath at McGilley's funeral parlor in Kansas City with a one-word note from Omar Bradley: "Thanks."

Edge of Understanding. Hal Boyle never owned a car or a house or a yacht or a country-club membership, but there were always friends ready to share these things with him. In one sense he was the world's worst weekend guest, because you could never be sure he would make it. When he did make it, he was the best.

He arrived with a bag full of compassion and charm for the hostess, and candy or gum for the kids. He also came with a supply of beguiling abstractions, or "murkyisms," as we called them in the office. A murkyism is a thought that hovers on the edge of understanding, one side or the other.

Once, with our youngest on his knee, he said, "Sukey, remember one thing. Be kind to your dear and true to your always."

She stared right back at him, just inches from his Botticelli-blue eyes, and said, "Mr. Boyle, that doesn't make any sense." But she knew, she knew, and he laughed loudly.

At the typewriter, Boyle was a study in concentration and terror, taut, silent, intense, measuring each word carefully for content and sound, writing, X-ing out, rephrasing, sweating out the sentences until finally they emerged with shining simplicity.

He wrote of many things. . . .

Of the first apartment he and Frances had, so tiny, so short of storage space "I had to mail my high-school-graduation book back to Mother."

Of his first experience in war. "In war, as in love, it is your first campaign that stays bone-deep in your memory. And Tunisia was our introduction to the sweetheart with the lipless kiss."

Of South Carolina and "a tar-papered shack wearying a

hill. . . ." Of the farm in Ireland, where his mother grew up, where "Irish pride jutted above the stones of Irish poverty."

Of trying futilely to tell his daughter Tracy she had been adopted. "Sometime, though, she will ask a question but not now. Not now."

Of a middle-aged columnist looking into the mirror on his birthday, searching for the boy and finding "all that was left of him was his eyes—two blue pools of doubt, two wells of childhood reluctant to cloud over. . . ."

On St. Patrick's Day in 1972, after friends had detected a slurring of speech, it appeared that Hal Boyle had had a slight stroke. He had to be persuaded to go to a hospital, and a friend, Jules Loh of the AP, went along. Boyle insisted on stopping for an Irish coffee. "After all, I'm going to miss the parade." Then they went to his apartment to get some clothes and books. Boyle was maddeningly meticulous, picking out just the right books, and Loh grew nervous. Then they had to stop for cigars. Then Hal said, "On danger's grave he planted freedom's flag."

"What's that mean?" asked Loh, who should have known better.

"I don't know, but wouldn't it look great on my tombstone?"

Nearing the hospital, Boyle said, "Before I die, I'd like to do one truly unselfish act."

"Like what, Hal?" Loh asked softly.

"Like rescue a banker's daughter from a runaway horse."

No friend in trouble, or simply with time to kill, ever found Boyle wanting. Money, time or, more precious, carefully considered advice were always forthcoming. He collected for office retirement parties. He missed no funerals or wakes, including his own.

"See You Later." Hal Boyle wrote his last column on February 21, 1974, the day after his 63rd birthday. In all the weeks since the previous November, when he began to live with the knowledge that he was dying, he had tried to keep the column going. But now even a neck brace could no longer keep his head up. His fingers, his arms, his energy had deserted him. He could no longer type.

And so he dictated his last column to me, slowly, evenly, softly. After writing some 7680 columns in more than 30 years, he said, it was time to slow down. "Like an old hen, I will lay fewer eggs and spend more time brooding."

There followed five paragraphs of charm and whimsey, and then he settled down to the real reason for giving up his column: "I became the first guy on my block to acquire a rare and little known malady—amyotrophic lateral sclerosis. It's a mysterious affliction of the spinal cord which cripples a body through atrophy of the voluntary muscles. The disease is progressive and terminal. The irony of it to me is that after surviving three wars without a scratch I come down with an ailment that on the average strikes only one out of every 100,000 people.

"I hate to relinquish my daily column because writing it has been more than bread and butter to me. It has been a magic adventure that enabled me to meet thousands of people, 67 countries and every continent but the Antarctic.

"I guess this is the place to express my deeply felt thanks to all the readers who through the years made the journey with me and shored up my spirits with kind letters of cheer, suggestion and criticism.

"See you later."

We went to lunch.

Back home, Margaret Gavaghan Boyle, 86, read her son's last column in the Kansas City *Star* and died three days later. Enfeebled by his disease, Hal flew home and stood there to the last moment with his sister and brothers. It was a completely draining time for a man who had so little strength left. But the only comment we got from Boyle on his return was: "You should've seen the huge wreath the office sent. You would've thought Momma had just won the Kentucky Derby."

Fate spared Hal the ultimate indignity of his disease. He died on April 1 of a heart attack.

He was also spared the conventional retirement party, with its gold watch and "mutualments and endearies," as he called them. At Hal's party, held just three days before he died, instead of a gold watch we gave him a belly dancer who popped out of a cardboard cake. We also gave him the news that his friends had established in his name a scholarship at the School of Journalism at the University of Missouri. To mark the occasion, the university presented him with a handsome pewter plate.

Hal said he was so impressed with the scholarship fund he

might contribute to it himself. And, as always, seeking to build a bridge between two worlds, he gave the pewter plate to the belly dancer.

Saga of the Chicken Colonel

by James Steward-Gordon

Col. Harland Sanders, of Louisville, Ky., the founding father, tireless promoter and international image of Kentucky Fried Chicken, is probably the best-known bewhiskered American since Abraham Lincoln. Aided by a $50-million-a-year advertising and publicity budget, the Colonel is as visible as the Statue of Liberty on a clear day. His goateed face beams out from highway billboards, the fronts of his stores, on television commercials and talk shows, and on the more than two million containers of Kentucky Fried Chicken sold every day. Summer or winter he sports a white suit, a string tie anchored by a diamond the size of a grape, black elastic-sided gaiters, and a cane. In his promotional travels, which in recent years were averaging 250,000 miles annually, he has worn out eight of those suits a year.

The Colonel's career is a saga of American independence

and grit colorful enough to be set to music and sung to banjo accompaniment. He formed Kentucky Fried Chicken in 1956 when he was a 66-year-old, $105-a-month beneficiary of Social Security. By 1975 the business was grossing over $1 billion a year, had 5300 stores in 39 countries and was selling almost a million chickens every 24 hours.

According to the Colonel, who rattles off chicken statistics the way movie press agents once announced starlets' measurements, KFC in 1975 would consume "seven percent of the ten billion pounds of federally inspected broilers marketed in the United States. Each of these birds will be about eight weeks old, weigh 2½ pounds and be divided into nine pieces which will be served as three portions." Moreover, each chicken would be cooked in a Colonel Sanders-designed pot and seasoned with Sanders' secret formula of 11 herbs and spices, known only to a handful of trusted associates.

While KFC has earned millions for the Colonel, it has also been very kind to large numbers of people associated with it. No fewer than 125 persons employed or franchised by KFC between the years 1964 and 1971—when the company was sold to Heublein Inc., the food and liquor conglomerate—also became millionaires. During that time, stock shares shot up from $15 to $500 each; and within a few years, an original investment of $5000 was worth $3 million. Among those who benefited were secretaries, salesmen and "just folks" who worked around the place.

While much of KFC's success has been due to shrewd promotion, the Colonel's insistence on quality and uniformity has obviously helped. His unspoiled palate—he neither smokes nor drinks—is so refined he can detect the slightest deviation in any dish. And no matter where he traveled, the Colonel would spend several days a week dropping in unannounced at KFC emporiums, "a-lickin' and a-tastin' and never bein' satisfied." Says the Colonel: "Whether in Cedar Rapids, Iowa, or Tokyo, Japan, I want my chicken to taste the way I prepare it with my own hands."

The Colonel (he was so designated by a Kentucky governor grateful for "his contributions to the state's cuisine") is as impressive in person as he is on billboards. He is slightly over six feet tall and weighs 208 pounds. At a distance, in his dazzling white suit, he looks like a benign polar bear.

The Colonel and his lady, Miss Claudia, live in Louisville, in a lovely home which inclines more toward comfort than grandeur. There the Colonel divides his time between his greenhouse and keeping an eye on the restaurant he founded several years ago, called Claudia Sanders, The Colonel's Lady Dinner House. He sometimes dines there, but he much prefers to do his own cooking in his own kitchen, and even here his eating tastes are marked with originality. He is as liable to cook himself a lobster for breakfast as to boil himself a passel of eggs. However much he eats during the day, his dinner hour is an invariable 5:30 p.m.

A farm boy, Harland Sanders was born in Henryville, Ind., in 1890. At the age of six, with the death of his father, young Harland, the eldest of three children, became cook, baby-sitter and all-around head of the household while his mother went out to work. By the time he was eight he was turning out whole menus of American delicacies.

His mother remarried when he was 12, and Harland then hired out as a farmhand. He later became a streetcar conductor and eventually went to Cuba as a soldier. Back in the United States, he began a 38-year marathon involving a bewildering variety of careers. By turns he worked as a railroad fireman, section hand, insurance agent, steamboat promoter, gaslight manufacturer, tire salesman and finally service-station operator in Corbin, Ky.

This last job brought Sanders his first taste of real success—at the age of 40. To eke out the meager profits he made from selling gas, he started preparing homemade snacks to serve hungry travelers. In a few years his snack service had grown into a café with more than a local reputation.

But success presented a problem: how could he cook decent fried chicken to order without making a customer wait half an hour? The answer came in 1939 when he bought a pressure cooker. Tinkering with this device, he invented a means of frying chicken in just eight minutes while preserving its flavor. He named the product Kentucky Fried Chicken—to distinguish it from restaurant-made "southern fried" chicken, which, he says, "isn't southern and more often than not tastes like wet cardboard."

In time the Sanders Café grew into a 142-seat enterprise, with a motel attached, valued at $164,000. Then disaster struck. In the mid 1950s, the two roads on which the restaurant stood were bypassed by new superhighways, and Sanders, whose place was isolated by the change, was forced to sell at auction for just enough to cover his debts. Faced with the prospect of trying to live on Social Security and his small savings, he struck out at the age of 66 for new frontiers.

Sanders' principal asset was his method of frying chicken. Loading up his 1946 Ford with a 50-pound can of seasoning and his beloved pressure cooker, he took to the road. "Let me cook chicken for you and your staff," he told restaurateurs. "If you like the way it tastes, I'll sell you my seasoning, teach you how to cook it, and you pay me a four-cent royalty on every chicken you sell."

Although business was slow at first, by 1960 Sanders had 400 franchises in the United States and Canada. It was during this time that he developed his distinctive style of dress. Asked to appear on a TV talk show in Colorado, he put on his only clean suit—a white Palm Beach. People immediately linked the suit and the words Kentucky Fried Chicken, and a national symbol was born. By 1964, there were 638 KFC outlets, grossing $37 million a year, and the Colonel had begun to mutter that "this danged business is beginning to run right over me."

When a 29-year-old Kentucky lawyer, John Young Brown, Jr., and a 60-year-old Nashville financier named Jack Massey offered him $2 million for the business, he agreed to sell all rights except to operations in Florida, Utah and Montana, plus Canada and England (he gave away or sold these rights himself). He also received a lifetime salary and was put in charge of quality control.

By 1968, Brown and Massey were spending $7 million a year advertising the Colonel and his chicken, and grossing $700 million in sales. Three years later, with the Colonel's agreement, they sold out to Heublein. Brown received $35 million in cash and stock for his share, and Massey slightly more. As for the Colonel, no one except the IRS knows for sure what his share of the profits has come to.

Today, despite his years and his wealth (which he is busily distributing through several foundations), the Colonel's two principal interests remain work and food. Up at five o'clock every morning, he is ready for work—after a session with a diathermy machine for his arthritic hands—by six. He visits his greenhouse and takes a brisk walk, then sets out on his numerous activities for the gigantic enterprise he has brought to life. Each year he travels to several foreign countries to bring them the opportunity of seeing the Colonel in the flesh.

When asked a few years ago why he kept working at the same pace as ever, the Colonel snorted. "Work never hurt anyone," he said. "More people rust out than wear out. But not me. I'll be damned if I'll *ever* rust out."

The Enemy of the Good

by Walter B. Pitkin

Henry Sherrard taught Greek in Detroit High School. He didn't have to teach school. He was a person of means who insisted on teaching only because he loved to teach. In appearance, as in personality, he was a freak. His six feet four inches of ill-clad, awkward height were topped by a red-brown thatch of untamed hair. From the unsymmetrical jumble of bones and teeth which formed his face shone blue eyes, nerve-racking in their penetration. His clothes were a clutter, thinly covered with chalk dust. He was a walking scarecrow, a myth in baggy pants.

When I fell into his hands I was 16, impressionable and eager to know things. He hammered at me for two solid years, as a blacksmith hammers on the anvil. For Sherrard was that rarest of humans, a perfectionist whose devotion to perfection was itself perfection. He was forever troubling the Board of Education and the other teachers because he wouldn't compromise. He had his own ideals of teaching, his own ways of pursuing them. And he would go his own way through hell and high water.

His favorite methods of teaching were contempt, intimidation, and a kick in the pants. He used these, however, only after the victim had received every opportunity to learn his lesson as Sherrard insisted it be learned—100 percent correctly.

Our first day in class Sherrard solemnly contemplated us for a long time. Then he said with the utmost gentleness: "So you want to learn Greek? Well, it's a praiseworthy ambition, but I hope you know what you're up against. I must explain. I am the Enemy of the Good."

A boy tittered nervously. Sherrard eyed him and went on.

"I am not joking. I do not like good students. I like only the best. I do not like a good translation. I like only the right translation.

"You either know something or you don't know it. You either can do a thing or you can't. I shall do my best to teach you Greek. But that forces me to see that you do your best to learn it.

"Now for procedure. Every day you must make a perfect score. You must pronounce perfectly. You must translate perfectly.

"To help you become perfect, I shall insist that you write on the blackboard, ten times over, the correction of every single mistake. If, after you have worked on a mistake thus, you again commit it, you will write the correction 100 times. And now let us begin Greek."

Thus started two decisive years of my life. Sherrard's game excited me. If one could be perfect, even in a small thing, might not one become perfect in another thing, and then another? In time one might be perfect in many things, and that would be marvelous.

Other pupils went to class trembling. I went as to a gladiatorial contest, to see the Christians thrown to the Lion. When the Lion rushed at me roaring, I grinned. Then the Lion winked. And I knew I was on the right track.

Sometimes, after I'd covered a blackboard with sentences, by way of correcting a wrong accent, I'd erase the stuff and do it all over again. This paralyzed the Lion. To think that anybody, driven to write something 10 times, would write it

20! If the Lion only knew that I used to go home and cover sheets of wrapping paper with Greek sentences, just to beat him at his own game!

He blue-penciled every least error in the papers we handed in daily. He wrote savage comments on bad blunders. He never overlooked one line. How he did it I cannot imagine. Yet he did it year in and year out, without faltering.

Our second year we attacked Homer. Every day five lines committed perfectly to memory, or else. . . . Every day we arose and sang off the first book from the opening line through the day's quota. One sloppy pronunciation and we had to begin all over, which grew irksome when you had to go back 200 lines.

I never had been able to learn prose or verse. I hated to recite set pieces. Something in me rebelled. But Henry Sherrard drove me through the first two books of the *Iliad*, line by line; and had me, at the year's close, intoning them complete, knowing every word I uttered and having the feel of the whole business, almost as if it were English.

Those who wouldn't play the game of perfection had a hard time. "So, Mr. Jones," Sherrard would leer at a sinner, "you do not seem to care whether the adjective agrees with its noun. If you leave quietly, Mr. Jones, and never show your face around here again, I'll not kick you. But go fast, Mr. Jones. Get a job unloading watermelons down at the docks. Watermelons don't have to agree with anything. Now get out, Mr. Jones, before I crack your skull."

But if a poor soul really did his utmost, Sherrard was courteous to the last. He understood when the will strained and the mind creaked like an overworked harness. He believed the weak should be treated humanely, and he sent such failures on their way to oblivion in a kindly manner. He'd lay his hand on the youth's shoulder, beam, ask him to look in sometime when he was passing, and bid him godspeed.

I played the game of perfection and won. But did Sherrard pat me on the back? Did he say: "Well done, young man"? He did not. You did a thing to perfection. How silly to praise you or it!

We read the last lines of the *Iliad* on a hot, sticky June day. Sherrard closed the book, looked out of the window, shuffled to the door, and was gone. I never saw him again.

But now, half a century later, I still measure people—teachers, pupils and others—according to his rule: "Whatever is worth doing at all is worth doing well. Whatever is worth doing well is worth doing perfectly."

I decided to study writing as I had studied Greek. Soon I was finishing, in a few minutes, daily themes on which we were supposed to spend hours. Next I took to writing themes for the lame ducks, to kill time. I tried the method of perfection on Hebrew, on Arabic, on sociology. Try sitting in an ordinary classroom after two years of Sherrard!

I have found two classes of men who were satisfied with nothing short of perfection—the truly great scientists who fight for accuracy down to the fifth decimal place, and the officers of the German General Staff. As a graduate student in Germany before World War I, I came to know several generals and many younger officers. They thought and lived as did Sherrard. Toward themselves they were as ruthless as toward subordinates. Either you know or you don't know. Either you can or you can't. If you don't know, or if you can't, then out with you!

As the German army overran France in 1940, I thought of Sherrard.

Everyone, at least once, ought to fall under the spell of a fanatical perfectionist. Only thus can the common man come to realize his own astounding possibilities. To watch a man completely devoted to the highest possible ideal is more than an education. It is like a religious conversion. To see in action a man who is the fierce enemy of the good because he loves only the best is to see the whole world in a fresh and startling light. To understand that it is possible to hate half-knowledge, half-skills, half-hearted ideals, sets fire to something inside you.

Our world perishes under the misleading of stupid people who disbelieve in perfection. Calling themselves realists, they are actually victims of the vulgar myth of man's supreme, invincible incompetence. Deeming people to be much worse than they are, these so-called leaders become compromisers, shirkers, or false liberals who spout words and choke on deeds.

"You can't make people perfect, or the world perfect," they object. But men, by trying to perfect themselves, their business and their government, may make all these 10 times better than they now are. Wouldn't that be worth the effort?

Forgotten is most of the Greek Sherrard taught me. But unforgettable is the passion for perfection that inhabited that sorry jumbled frame of a man. Ten thousand years after I have gone, that strange fire will be burning in other races and peoples. If it dies out, man will be no more.

Ritz Is the Word For Elegance

by George Kent

When you put on the ritz, or describe something as ritzy, you are paying tribute to a Swiss peasant whose education never took him beyond simple arithmetic. His name, in every Western language, has become a synonym for luxury. The story of César Ritz is the story of a genius who did much to transform hotel living into an art. You will find his mark on every continent today, wherever a hotel puts an accent on grace, comfort and imaginative good taste.

Ritz lived at the turn of the century, when women were beginning to demand equality. He encouraged them, helped bring them out of their Victorian cloisters. When he arrived in London in the late '90s, for example, no woman of good family would dare be seen dining in public. Ritz persuaded a few great ladies—like the Duchess of Devonshire and Lady Dudley—to come to his hotel dining rooms. Others followed, and soon dining at the Savoy, Carlton, Claridge's or Ritz—all owned or managed by Ritz at one time or another—became a social must.

Ritz introduced soft lighting to flatter women's complexions and show their gowns to best advantage. He planned his dining rooms so that women, mounting a short flight of stairs, could make an "entrance." He conspired with his famous chef, Auguste Escoffier, to create scores of dishes that would appeal especially to women. And he presented dinner music—for the first time in London. Always the perfectionist, he chose the orchestra of Johann Strauss to play for his guests.

César Ritz was born in the Swiss mountain village of Niederwald, and went to work at 16 in a hotel dining room in the nearby town of Brieg. A few months later he was discharged. "In the hotel business," commented his employer, "you need an aptitude—a flair. You haven't a trace of it."

Ritz got another job as a waiter—and again was booted out. He went to Paris, where he got—and lost—two more jobs. His career really began with the fifth job, in a chic little restaurant near the Madeleine where he climbed from bus boy to waiter and finally to manager. He was still only 19 when his employer invited him to become his partner. To any other young fellow this might have been a wonderful opportunity. But Ritz knew now what he wanted: the world of great names, of epicurean feasts.

Rolling up his aprons, he walked down the street to the No. 1 restaurant of the day, Voisin's, and went to work as an assistant waiter, once more at the bottom. He watched and learned—how to press a duck and carve a roast; how to decant a Burgundy; how to serve food in a way that pleased the eye as well as the palate. Everybody dined at Voisin's: Sarah Bernhardt, Alexandre Dumas the younger, the Rothschilds.

In 1871 Ritz left Paris and for three years worked in fashionable resort restaurants in Germany and Switzerland. There opportunity twisted the doorknob.

He was by then restaurant manager of the Rigi-Kulm, an Alpine hotel noted for its view and its cuisine. One day the heating plant broke down. Almost at the same moment a message arrived—40 wealthy Americans were on their way for lunch!

The temperature of the dining room was down around freezing. Ritz, wrapped in an overcoat, ordered the lunch table set up in the drawing room—it had red curtains and *looked* warmer. Into four huge copper pots, employed until then for holding palm trees, he poured alcohol and set it ablaze. Bricks were put into the ovens.

When the guests arrived the room was tolerably warm, and under the feet of each diner went a hot brick wrapped in flannel. The meal was a cold-weather masterpiece, starting with a peppery hot consommé and ending with flaming crêpes suzette. The party, warm without and within, departed chanting the praises of the young manager.

This small miracle of quick thinking was gossiped about wherever hotelmen gathered. Finally it reached the ears of the owner of a large hotel in Lucerne that was steadily losing money. He asked Ritz to become general manager.

In two years the 27-year-old peasant put the hotel on a paying basis. Here he developed the methods we associate with his name. For Ritz no detail was too picayune, no enterprise too large if it meant the happiness of a guest.

"People like to be served," Ritz used to say, "but *invisibly*." The rules he formulated are the four commandments of a good hotelkeeper today: to see all without looking; to hear all without listening; to be attentive without being servile; to anticipate without being presumptuous.

"The customer is always right," he said to a waiter, using that now-hackneyed phrase for the first time. If a guest complained of the size of a bill he smiled genially, took it away and forgot to bring it back. If the diner did not like the meat or the wine it was whisked from the table. Ritz had a prodigious memory. He remembered who liked a certain brand of Turkish cigarettes, who had a passion for chutney—and when they arrived these things were waiting for them.

He also catered to his more permanent guests. The tall man found an eight-foot bed in his room. Mrs. Smith, who could not bear flowers, was never annoyed with them but Mrs. Jones, who loved gardenias, always found a bowl of them on her breakfast tray.

Ritz combined the imagination of an impresario with his other talents. When the Princess Caroline de Bourbon told him he could have carte blanche in arranging a fete at Lucerne to celebrate her engagement, he produced a party that is still talked about. Waiting at the edge of the lake were 12 beflowered and illuminated sailboats, and as each guest came aboard, a sailor at the stern let go with Roman candles. Large boats moved among the smaller craft serving food and drink. On the four peaks that look down on the lake huge bonfires sprang to life.

In 1892 Ritz went to London to take over the financially tottering Hotel Savoy. With Escoffier in the kitchen and César everywhere, the public responded and the hotel was out of the red in an astonishingly short time. Roving from room to room Ritz remade beds to be sure they were right; once, inspecting the dining room, he smelled soap on a glass and sent several hundred glasses back to be rewashed.

He was doing over the decorations of a bridal suite one day, and the bronze chandelier protruding from the ceiling offended him. As he looked for a way to light the room less obtrusively, the projecting cornices gave him an idea. He put the lights back of them—and indirect lighting was introduced.

Arranging a party for Alfred Beit, the South African diamond king, Ritz flooded the Savoy ballroom, transformed it into a miniature Venice. Guests were served as they reclined in gondolas. Caruso sang to a gathering which included Cecil Rhodes, James Gordon Bennett, Gilbert and Sullivan, Lord Randolph Churchill.

Ritz had a puckish sense of humor and occasionally played jokes on his guests. One victim—also one of his greatest admirers—was the Prince of Wales, later King Edward VII. Ritz served him a dish he called *Cuisses de Nymphes à l'Aurore*—Thighs of Nymphs at Dawn. His Royal Highness loved it. Later in the evening he learned that the dish was frogs' legs, served with cream and Moselle wine—the Prince detested frogs' legs.

Ritz's golden era at the Savoy ended with a quarrel between him and the directors. Ritz walked out. The reaction among César's friends was instantaneous. From the Prince of Wales came the statement: "Where Ritz goes, we follow." More than

200 messages expressing similar sentiments arrived within a week.

Now he returned to his beloved Paris and realized a dream he had cherished for years: he established, in the Place Vendôme, the grandest of all Ritz hotels. To discourage idlers he planned a small lobby. To encourage conversation over tea or coffee he designed a garden. Wanting cleanliness, he painted the walls instead of papering them because paint could be washed. For the design of his furniture he went to Versailles and Fontainebleau. The color scheme he borrowed from a painting by Van Dyck.

An innovation was the number of rooms equipped with private baths. On the day of the opening people streamed through the corridors as through a museum, largely to inspect the bathrooms.

The success of the Ritz of Paris was never in doubt. On one dinner menu preserved by an old Ritz employee were the autographs of four kings, seven princes and assorted nobility. Among Americans who lived and dined there were John Pierpont Morgan, Jay Gould, Commodore Vanderbilt, John Wanamaker. The British contingent included Lord Northcliffe, Nellie Melba, Lily Langtry. On all Ritz lavished his extraordinary attention, sensitive to every mood and price.

Here Ritz fixed the traditional waiter's costume: white tie for the waiter, black tie for the maître d'hôtel. He also gave the bellhop his brass buttons.

At the turn of the century Ritz built and opened the Carlton Hotel in London, and a few years later came the hotel in Piccadilly which bears his name. The latter was the first building in England to use steelframe construction, which Ritz, enamored of the Eiffel Tower, had insisted on. A group of financiers joined with Ritz to create the Ritz Hotel Development Corp., which produced most of the Ritz hotels scattered through the world. One of these was the Ritz-Carlton of New York.

In 1902 Ritz prepared a huge dinner and reception in honor of the coronation of Edward VII. Arrangements were complete to the final detail when word came that the King was seriously ill and required an immediate operation. Ritz attended to all the details of the dismantling and cancellation, and then collapsed. It was a mental attack from which he never recovered.

As he lay dying, in October 1918, he murmured, thinking his wife was at his side, "Take care of our daughter." They had two sons, but no girl. Between them, "daughter" was the way they referred to the Ritz Hotel in Paris.

"I'm Doc's Kid"

by Helen Graham Rezatto

"I've got to make a call," Doc Lynde said to me. "Want to come along?"

"Oh, yes, Doc!" I cried. All the kids in Ellendale, N.D., vied to accompany Doc on his rounds and this time I, a ten-year-old, had beaten out the teen-agers.

I delivered the exciting news at home and raced back to Doc's garage. Dr. Roy Lynde loved medicine and machinery in about equal parts, and with his brother Guy had the town's Plymouth-Chrysler agency. It was a two-story brick building with salesroom and service garage on the first floor, Doc Lynde's office and bachelor living quarters on the second.

Doc was waiting for me, and off we rolled over the flat farmlands toward the Coteau-Missouri hills. This was the fall of 1930, and the land was in the grip of the great drought. As we drove through the desolate countryside I saw endless drifts of dust, once topsoil, piled against the fences. Sometimes grass-

177

hoppers blanketed the road, and as we drove over them we'd hear a crisp crackling sound and the car would skid a bit. We talked about the drought, about school and the teachers, about the football team. I talked as if he were ten years old and he talked as if I were 55. We understood each other perfectly.

Finally we turned in at a farmhouse, and out of it came a man and woman in faded, patched clothes. Inside we found a boy, about my age, in bed. His face, terribly pale because of a blood disease, lit up when he saw us. Doc took his temperature, thumped and poked him, all the time talking about a baseball game he'd seen recently. Finally he poured some pills into an envelope and handed them to the anxious mother.

"You know what's gonna fix you up?" Doc said to the boy. "Frog spit." The boy let out a whoop of delight. "You do what your mom tells you, and when you're strong enough to get outdoors, then you get some frog spit on the middle finger of your right hand, and you'll be fit as a fiddle."

As we were going out through the kitchen I saw the farmer reach up on a shelf for a Mason jar half full of coins. Doc saw this, too, and hustled me out of the door. "Next time," he called over his shoulder. "Next time."

As we roared away Doc grumped, "The damn fool. Last money he had in the world and he wanted to give it away."

Strangers sometimes thought Doc Lynde was a grouch. True, there was a downward set to his mouth and a bulldog thrust to his chin and he said "hell" and "damn" a good deal, two words not generally employed in our Lutheran and Methodist town. But all you had to do was look at his eyes to see the merriment inside. He was every kid's friend, and the grownups' too.

Doc didn't have office hours; he was available around the clock. The 1900 people in Ellendale went to bed early, but at any hour of the night in the darkened town you could find one square of light: Doc's window. It told us that he was sleeping lightly, ready to respond to any need. It gave everyone a feeling of security.

Realizing that his appearance at a bedside was good medicine, Doc would make a house call no matter what the distance or difficulties. I remember one January day during a terrible blizzard when the county road foreman stomped into my father's law office, shaking his head in disbelief. "You know what Doc just did? He came into the highway garage and said he had to make a call at the Schmidt farm and wanted me to plow him a way to it. I told him that's a back road and I've got barely enough men to keep the county roads open. Next thing I knew he jumped into one of the plows and took off into the storm. He's got 20 miles to go and he's never handled a snowplow."

"He'll make it," my father said.

He did. And he made it in another storm, too, a few winters later. That time he borrowed a handcar and we watched him head down the railroad tracks, pumping for all he was worth, to see a sick man in the north part of the county. It was midnight before he got home, by the same method.

Doc's bedside manner was unique. He'd enter the sick room cracking jokes or telling stories, and never give the patient a chance to list his complaints. But all during his monologue he would carefully probe, touch, look, analyze. His theory was that if he ever appeared to take the symptoms seriously, the patient would imagine that he was sicker than he really was.

Actually, Doc's diagnostic skill was amazing, and he was ahead of his time in treatment. He massaged polio victims before Sister Kenny was heard of, and he gave thrombosis patients limited exercise when the rest of the country was giving only bed rest. Hypochondriacs and malingerers received short shrift, however. "Damn it," he'd say to a patient. "I wish *I* had your heart."

The Lyndes' garage was an after-school hangout for kids. We delighted in the practical jokes Doc and his cronies played on one another. We laughed when they laughed, and felt grown-up. Doc always treated us as if we had good sense and opinions that deserved an audience.

The town's No. 1 sports fan, Doc didn't miss a single high-school game if he could help it. When the games were out of town, he'd pile his car full of kids and off we'd go to cheer for Ellendale. When we grew older, Doc would loan us brand-new cars out of the showroom for joy rides and out-of-town games. (He carried special insurance to cover this.) He never said, "Be careful." He said, "Take her out and see if she's any good." And because he assumed we were responsible, we were.

I never had an accident with one of Doc's cars, but I did with my father's. I wrinkled a fender against a telephone pole, then drove the car to Doc's garage and broke into tears.

"Hell," he said. "You didn't do much damage. We can fix that so your dad will never know."

He and Alvin, his mechanic, went to work on that fender and it came out smooth and shiny, and Dad never did know. No charge, of course.

Ray's Café was another hangout, where we went for sodas after school. Whenever Doc happened to drop in, every booth would set up a clamor for him to sit there. One time he paused before the booth where I was jammed in with seven other girls, looked directly at me (I thought) and said, "Damn funny thing. All the kids I deliver turn out to be the best-looking."

I blushed with pleasure and pride, then suddenly realized that every girl in the booth had been delivered by him. Still, we each took it personally.

My first really objective view of Doc came after I had gone away to college and returned home for Thanksgiving vacation. Visiting his office, I observed his habit of dipping the thermometer in alcohol, then wiping it on his necktie before putting it in a patient's mouth, and noticed how he allowed Tom, his big striped cat, to sleep in the baby incubator when it was not in use. So what? Nobody ever got sick from the germs on Doc's tie, and no baby objected to Tom's use of the incubator.

I made a few country calls with Doc, but now he had a new system of priorities: any medical student who was home vacationing had first rights. At least ten boys from Ellendale were becoming, or had become, doctors because of Doc's inspiration—and often with the help of his cash. Kenneth Leiby was one of the medical students that fall. One morning as I was talking with Ken's mother, Doc's car came down the street. Ken was with him and his face was split with a triumphant grin. Even Doc was allowing himself a small Cheshire-cat smile. Ken jumped out of the car and came racing toward us.

"Do you know what happened?" he cried. "We went on this OB case about 50 miles out in the country, and she delivered at about six this morning. Well, Doc has the baby up by the heels and is spanking some wind into it when he turns to me and says, 'I got mine, now go get yours.' Gee, she was having twins—and I delivered a baby! What do you think of *that?*"

We thought it was pretty wonderful, and no one was prouder than Doc.

After college I married, and in 1943 my husband went off to war leaving me in New York, pregnant. I went to an immaculate, efficient obstetrician with a starched nurse and gleaming equipment, and I hated every minute of it. I wanted an old, cluttered medical office over a garage. I went home. Doc Lynde had delivered me, and it was he who delivered my baby son. With my husband away, it gave me a comforting sense of the continuity of life.

Doc was always there when needed. One afternoon while my father was working in the garden he had a heart attack. Doc was at our house in minutes and this time there were no jokes. Crisply he ordered me, "Run down to the garage and tell Alvin to bring the oxygen tank, the one we've been using to weld broken springs."

When we returned with the tank we found that Doc and my mother had improvised a tent with bed sheets draped over the fourposter and pinned down to the mattress. He inserted the valve of the oxygen tank under the sheets and began turning it on and off by hand. This makeshift arrangement needed constant attention and Doc was on his knees with it for four hours straight. He saved my father's life. It was this kind of devotion he gave to every sick man and woman and child in the county.

Despite other heart attacks, my father lived an active life for nine more years. Then even Doc Lynde could do no more. After my father's funeral the family returned to the bleakness of an empty house. Each sat with his own heavy burden of loss. Suddenly up the sidewalk came Doc. He entered the room briskly, tossed his hat and coat in a corner and said, "Well now, that was a mighty fine speech the minister made about Fred. Don't you think so?"

The text had been from Timothy: "I have fought a good fight, I have finished my course, I have kept the faith." Doc grinned at us. "Now, you can't deny it, Fred did have some good fights."

My father had indeed been a strong-willed, rugged individualist. Doc now began to recall his more notable legal and political battles, and we found ourselves smiling, and laughing. Soon we were immersed in wonderful, sustaining memories of the living man. Doc helped us through that first day without our even realizing that we were his patients, that he was prescribing the potent medicine of good memories.

It took our town a long time to discover that Doc was growing old. He was so much a part of our daily lives that we failed to notice the slow accumulation of wrinkles on his face, or that he paused more and more frequently to catch his breath. It was hard to face the fact that one day the beacon light on the second floor of the garage would be extinguished.

Suddenly we all wanted to express to Doc how we felt about him. But how? Then someone thought of giving him a surprise party on his 76th birthday. On that evening he was taken out for an automobile ride. As the car approached the high school Doc saw the drum majorettes standing by the gym and he exclaimed, "Damn it, have I forgotten a game?"

His host suggested they stop and find out. As Doc stepped from the car the majorettes surrounded him and escorted him in. A mighty roar went up from the residents of Ellendale and Dickey County, and then the throng burst into "Happy Birthday." Doc looked stunned and glanced behind him as if to escape, but the drum majorettes were between him and the door. With a sheepish grin on his weather-beaten face, he took the place of honor at the head table.

There were skits, speeches and gifts. Dr. Kenneth Leiby, the boy who had delivered the twins with Doc and was now a successful general practitioner in New Hope, Pa., had commissioned a large oil portrait of Doc, painted from photographs, which he now presented to the community.

At one point during the speeches the toastmaster said, "Of course, since Doc is a bachelor he has no kids."

"I'm Doc's kid," squeaked a three-year-old, jumping up.

"I'm Doc's kid," called out a young housewife, standing.

"I'm Doc's kid," boomed the town newspaper editor, rising to his feet.

One by one, people identified themselves until there was a great throng standing. They looked at Doc and he looked back at them and suddenly his chin began to quiver. We had found a way to thank him. Our very existence was our tribute to his skilled and loving hands.

We tried to honor Doc in other ways. We built the Dr. Roy Lynde Memorial Nursery section of the county hospital. On the 50th anniversary of the day he began medical practice after graduating from the University of Minnesota, we held a civic holiday with a parade and a double-header during which we dedicated the ball park as the Dr. Roy Lynde Memorial Athletic Field.

As I write this, he is 86. The dust in his office is undisturbed, for his instruments are now relics of the past. When he leaves the garage to go to the restaurant for dinner he walks very slowly and, should he falter, a dozen people are at his side. Each night a different neighbor looks in on him to be certain he's all right. During the week the population of Ellendale parades past his chair in the garage just to say, "Hi, Doc." The mighty force of the love he has given others over the years now returns to range protectively around him.

I look at him and think of all the sick people he's held in his arms, the bills he's forgotten, the jokes he's laughed at, the kids he's spoiled, the kind deeds he's hidden. And I think of the richness he's brought to our town. Each of us has tried to be a little bit like Doc. None of us made it all the way, but we're more understanding and generous and loving than we would have been if he hadn't lived among us.

Could any man hope to accomplish more?

Sports and Adventure

Behind the Legend of Babe Ruth

by Roger Kahn

In his time and in his way, George Herman Ruth was a holy sinner. He was a man of measureless lust, selfishness and appetites, but he was also a man undyingly faithful, in a manner, to both his public and his game.

Ruth died on August 16, 1948. After the funeral service, as a great crowd stood in reverent silence, pallbearers, many of them Ruth's own teammates, carried the casket into the fierce heat of the summer day.

"Lord," whispered Joe Dugan, the Yankee third baseman during Ruth's prime, "I'd give my right arm for an ice-cold beer." Waite Hoyt, the former pitcher, turned slightly. "Joe," he murmured, "so would The Babe."

The aging men who spent their youth playing side by side with Ruth remember. They remember more clearly than the writers who traveled with him or the fans who watched him;

187

even more clearly, perhaps, than the adopted daughters and the wife who loved him most. For they knew him in the camaraderie of strong, successful men, where no man passed verdict on the other, but where everyone knew The Babe was at once the strongest and most successful.

Facts and Fancy. Ruth lived for 53 years, but his special time was the 15 seasons he played for the New York Yankees. In the 1920s, the country teemed with sports figures whose names meant immediate idolatry: Bill Tilden and Red Grange, Knute Rockne and Jack Dempsey, Ty Cobb and Bobby Jones. Yet no one gathered and awed so many crowds for so many years as the man the whole nation called The Babe.

There is a curious derivative of Gresham's law that applies to American heroes. Just as bad money drives out good, so heroic fancy drives out heroic fact, and we are often left wondering what our man actually was like. The greater the hero, the more prevalent the fictions.

But to begin with, everything you have ever heard about Ruth on a baseball field is probably the truth or close to it. He could hit a baseball higher, farther and more dramatically than anyone else. His record of 60 home runs in a 154-game season is unquestionably the classic of all sports standards. His great swing, even when he struck out, was more awesome than the stroke of a lesser man which happened to produce a home run. He does seem always to have made the right play in the outfield. He did have superlative baseball instincts. More assuredly than anything else, he was the savior baseball had to find after the Chicago White Sox dumped the 1919 World Series. All these are part of the legend, and all ring true.

But once the stories of Ruth move off the diamond, fact fades away and dies. He liked children, but his life was not a priestly dedication to healing sick boys. He liked jokes, but his humor at best was coarse. He was devoutly religious, but only sporadically. He may not have been an utter social boor, but he was something less than tactful, something less than gracious, and something very much less than sensitive.

Once, when he accidentally spiked a Yankee named Ray Morehart, he apologized profusely, then said to a veteran, "Hey, when that guy join the club? Last week?" Morehart had been with the club for months. Ruth simply hadn't noticed.

"A Bad Kid." Babe Ruth, a huge, ignorant, sentimental emperor, was the product of a childhood so bleak it was almost no childhood at all. Then, in his early manhood, he found himself earning considerably more money and possessing far more popularity than the President of the United States. He was not humble in his change of fortune.

One day, when Calvin Coolidge went to a ball game, the Yankees were lined up for formal introductions. "How do you do, Mr. President," said one. "Good day, sir," said another.

Coolidge was walking slowly, shaking hands with each of the players, and Ruth, as he waited, took off his cap and wiped his forehead with a handkerchief.

"Mr. Ruth," President Coolidge said.

"Hot as hell, ain't it, Prez?" Mr. Ruth said.

Ruth appeared on the American scene through the modest gateway of Baltimore, where he was born in 1895, one of a number of children with whom the union of Kate Shamborg and G.H. Ruth, Sr., was blessed. Like W.C. Fields, he never tasted liquor before he was six. He also chewed tobacco and appears to have stolen whatever loose change his parents left about the house. "I was a bad kid," Ruth himself said afterward.

In 1902, when he was seven, Ruth was placed in St. Mary's Industrial School as an incorrigible. At St. Mary's, Ruth was taught to read and to write, schooled in the crafts of tailoring and shirtmaking and, in his spare hours, he played baseball. No one ever had to teach him baseball. Ruth was the ultimate natural. At 19, St. Mary's released him to the Baltimore Orioles, who were then in the International League, and, staggered by a $600-a-year contract, Ruth went forth into the world. He was a babe; the nickname came quickly and logically.

Four for Four. Within two seasons, he was starring as pitcher and pinch-hitter for the Boston Red Sox. In eight matches with Walter Johnson, the finest of modern American League pitchers, Ruth won six, three by scores of 1 to 0 and once when his homer provided the only run. In World Series competition, he pitched 29 consecutive scoreless innings. Ruth was a superb left-hander. He moved into the outfield for Boston in 1919 only because his pinch-hitting was so effective that he could earn more playing every day.

In 1920, the Yankees purchased Ruth for $100,000 in what

was the biggest of baseball deals up to that time. Dividends were prompt. In his first season with the Yankees, Ruth hit 54 home runs, almost double the old record and an achievement beyond belief to fans accustomed to home-run champions with totals of 10 or 12. Abruptly, Ruth was the wonder of baseball. The fans recognized it and so did Ruth.

This is what he did. Led the American League in homers every year but one in the decade. Led the Yankees into seven World Series. Drew a salary that went in rapid stages to $52,000 to $70,000 to $80,000. Provided the gate appeal that created Yankee Stadium. Rebuilt the game, which had been scientific, into an extension of his own slugging style.

And this is how he played his role. One day in 1924 (46 homers for The Babe), as dawn appeared over eastern Philadelphia, Ruth was sitting in an after-hours club, a girl on each knee, after a night of partying. Someone suggested it was time to leave. Ruth held an open bottle of champagne upside down over his head. "I ain't gonna be leaving for a while yet," he said.

At the ball park that afternoon, Ruth announced, "I feel real good."

"You don't look real good," said teammate Fred Merkle.

"I'll hit one," Ruth said.

"Bet?"

"A hundred."

"Wait a minute," Merkle said. "This is an easy park."

"All right," Ruth said. "I'll give you two-to-one."

On his first time at bat, Ruth walloped an outside pitch into the left-field stands. Then he lined a triple to right, crashed a triple in center and pulled a homer over the right-field wall. He had gone four for four without benefit of bed rest.

Called Out. To George Herman Ruth, women, money and alcohol were equally important. In 1914, he married a Texas girl named Helen Woodford, but a few years later they separated. The first Mrs. Ruth died in 1929. Ruth then married a former actress named Claire Hodgson, to whom, despite her continual efforts to tame him, he remained deeply attached. Still, Ruth was more than a two-woman man.

Not surprisingly, people were always trying to reform him.

Miller Huggins, the diminutive old pro who managed the Yankees, tried—first gently, then severely, and ultimately with a $5000 fine for breaking training. Ruth responded by holding Huggins at arm's length off the rear car of a speeding train. Claire Ruth succeeded somewhat in slowing her husband's pace, and Christy Walsh, Ruth's agent, finally did convince Ruth that his $80,000 income would not long endure. Trust funds set up by Walsh and an attorney helped Ruth live out his years in comfort.

But the later years were not bright. Ruth wanted to manage in the majors, and the Yankees offered him their farm team in Newark. "You can't take care of yourself," said Col. Jake Ruppert, one of the Yankees owners. "How can I be sure you can take care of my best players? Newark, Ruth, or nothing."

"Nothing," Ruth said.

In 1938, he was hired as a coach by the Dodgers. But that winter Leo Durocher, whose principal gift in Ruth's view was a quick tongue, was appointed Brooklyn manager. Ruth resigned, and was out of baseball for all time.

"He Was a God." He lived in a large apartment on Manhattan's Riverside Drive, and occupied his days with golf, fishing and watching baseball. Once he spoke at the Baseball Writers' dinner in New York. "I gave 22 years of my life to big-league baseball," he said, "and I'm ready to give 25 more." Nearly a thousand baseball men heard him. No one offered him a job.

Yet, till the end, Ruth the man and Ruth the legend grew. Anywhere he wandered he was The Babe, unique, unrivaled, unchallenged. What made him happy was that children knew him. He loved children genuinely, as well might a man who had no childhood of his own.

Cancer struck him in 1946, and he faced death, for two agonizing years, with utter disbelief. Dugan saw him when Ruth was confined to a wheelchair. "Joe," Ruth said, his voice cut to a whisper by the cancer. "Joe," he said, caught in the final horror of truth. "I'm gone, Joe. I'm gone." Dugan clutched his old friend's hand, and the two men wept. A few days later, Ruth was dead.

"To understand him," says Dugan, who probably knew The

Babe better than any man alive, "you had to understand he wasn't human. He was an animal. No human could have done the things he did and lived the way he did and been a ball player. You got to figure he was more than animal even. There never was anyone like him. He was a god."

Let the memory ring true, down to the last home run, down to the last bacchanal, through a small corridor of time.

Most Daring
Woman on Earth

by Phil Bowie

High on the roof of a six-story building, a woman struggled frantically with a man who was determined to fling her to her death. Forced closer and closer to the edge, she lost her footing and pitched over the side. In desperation, she twisted . . . falling . . . clawing . . . and caught the roof ledge with her hands.

Kitty O'Neil was performing a routine stunt for an episode in the TV series "Baretta." Working as a double for other actresses, she has performed similar heart-stoppers in many other TV and movie sequences. For the NBC special "Superstunt" in 1977, she performed a stunt which set two records for women: the longest fall (112 feet) and the highest ever attempted while afire.

Kitty is also the only woman ever to do a "cannon-car rollover," a stunt in which an explosive device is used to flip over a moving vehicle. And she is one of the few women ever to do a fully engulfed "fire gag." For this, she dresses in a protective suit, which is smeared with glue and set aflame. The temperature within her suit reaches at least 200 degrees F. before the flames are extinguished.

Kitty, age 34, doesn't look like the most sought-after stunt woman in Hollywood. A petite five-foot-two, she weighs a mere 97 pounds. There is a hint of mischief in her blue-green eyes, and only a suggestion of her grace and agility in the way she tosses her dark-brown hair. Because Kitty speaks in an off-pitch slur, most people who meet her suspect that she has a minor speech impediment. The fact is that she has been totally deaf since infancy.

She was four months old when concurrent attacks of measles, mumps and chicken pox destroyed her hearing. Resolved that her daughter would lead a normal life, Kitty's mother, a full-blooded Cherokee, went through the University of Texas to learn how to reach and teach her child.* Then she began the tedious process of coaxing four senses to fill the void left by the useless fifth.

"She taught me to swim and to respond to directions when I was a baby," Kitty says. "Then she taught me how to read lips and speak." (Her mother went on to teach other children with hearing defects, and eventually established the School of Listening Eyes in Wichita Falls, Texas.)

Kitty entered the public-school system in the third grade and at once earned good marks. At her mother's urging, she took piano lessons. She also learned to play the cello, enjoying the resonant vibrations and keeping her notes true by "feel."

At 12, she took up competitive swimming and developed an interest in diving. But because hearing and balance are so closely related, her instructors doubted she would ever be capable of the precise aerial acrobatics necessary to compete as a diver.

She surprised them and herself, though, at a swimming meet in Oklahoma. "One of our team's divers didn't show up," Kitty recalls. "On impulse I asked the coach to let me try." She captured first place.

She went on to win the Southwest District Junior Olympic diving title and came to the attention of Dr. Sammy Lee, a

*Kitty's father died in a plane crash when she was very young.

two-time Olympic diving champion, who coached exceptionally talented young divers in Anaheim, Calif.

At 16, Kitty moved to Anaheim to study with Dr. Lee. She attended high school in the morning, endured four rigorous hours of diving training each afternoon and studied in the evenings. Lee was impressed by her strength and stubborn determination, but he winced each time she slapped into the water wrong, at about 35 m.p.h., after leaping from the ten-meter (32-foot, 10-inch) platform. For months she wore ugly, pie-size bruises, but she shrugged off the punishment.

Kitty once told a reporter, a bit defiantly: "I can do anything. I like to do things people say I can't do because I'm deaf. I have to work harder than some, but look at the fun I have proving they're wrong."

In 1964, she placed twelfth in the U.S. team trials for the Tokyo Olympics. Then, after winning 38 blue ribbons, 17 first-place trophies and 31 gold medals in her diving career, she began exploring the entire world of sports—the more dangerous an endeavor, the more irresistible it was to her. "I guess I like danger," she told me, "and thrills. But mostly I want always to have a goal, some dream that I can try for."

She raced boats, drag cars and production sports cars. She tried sky diving, scuba diving and high-speed water skiing. In 1970, she set an official world's record as the fastest woman water-skier—at a phenomenal 104.85 m.p.h.

She also entered grueling off-road automobile and dune-buggy events. Cross-county motorcycle racing looked challenging, so Kitty soon achieved an expert rating and became the only woman in the world qualified for world speed record competition.

At a motorcycle meet in California in 1971, she met a competitor named Duffy Hambleton. "She was unbelievable," Duffy recalls. "I couldn't imagine being able to ride a motorcycle the way she could without hearing what gear the bike was in, or knowing when a competitor was coming up behind her." The admiration was mutual. Within a year, Kitty and Duffy were married.

Kitty settled down for the first few years of marriage, but the routine life eventually became boring. As a member of Stunts Unlimited, a fraternal organization of Hollywood's top stunt men, Duffy was risking hs neck regularly in movies and TV episodes.

"Kitty was getting restless," Duffy recalls, "so I asked her what she'd like to do. She said, 'Well, why don't I just do what you do? Teach me how to do stunts.' So we began teaching her how to fall and fake a fight and roll a car. When she began actually doing all of it, she really razzled and dazzled them!" Shortly thereafter, Kitty began stunting on various TV shows such as "Bionic Woman" and "Police Woman." In no time, she was receiving so many job offers that she had to turn many of them down.

Having taken on, and conquered, an assortment of stunts and sports, many of which have traditionally been dominated by men, Kitty next decided to go after the World Land Speed Record for women—308.56 m.p.h. In September 1976, in a test run on a dry lake in California, she drove a 38-foot, three-wheeled, rocket-powered land missile to an estimated 358 m.p.h. She was ready to make it official on a longer course. Dry Lake Alvord, in the desolate high desert of southeastern Oregon, was the site for her official run. It was the first week in December and winter was threatening to close in, but the lake offered a course about 11 miles long and relatively smooth.

On December 4, Kitty donned her driving suit and helmet, folded herself into the cockpit, fired up the car's 48,000-horsepower engine and arrowed toward the first of the photocell beams that would time her pass through the measured course. Within seconds, the car was only a speck on the horizon.

Two runs are required in opposite directions within two hours, to eliminate any advantage derived from wind or slope. An official speed is the average of the two runs through the timing traps. At the end of the first run, the engineers quickly turned the vehicle around, refueled it and checked all systems. Again Kitty roared away, the acceleration pressing her back in her bucket seat. A few minutes after she had coasted to a stop, the referee announced an average speed of 322 m.p.h.

But Kitty wanted to go faster, to set a record that would stand for some time. On December 6, she blasted to a new average speed of 512.706 m.p.h. It took her more than five miles just to stop. Kitty had become the fastest woman on earth.

Kitty would like to edge her record still higher. If she had her way, she would go for the sound barrier itself (approximately 738 m.p.h.). If she does, it will be the second time for her. She has already overcome a sound barrier in her own life.

JOHN BAKER'S LAST RACE

by William J. Buchanan

The future looked bright to 24-year-old John Baker in the spring of 1969. At the peak of an astonishing athletic career, touted by sportswriters as one of the fastest milers in the world, he had fixed his dreams on representing the United States in the 1972 Olympic Games.

Nothing in Baker's early years had hinted at such prominence. Slight of build, and inches shorter than most of his teenage Albuquerque pals, he was considered "too uncoordinated" to run track in high school. But something happened during his junior year that changed the course of his life.

For some time, the Manzano High track coach, Bill Wolffarth, had been trying to induce a tall, promising runner named John Haaland—who was Baker's best friend—to join the track team. Haaland refused. "Let *me* join the team," Baker suggested one day. "Then Haaland might, too." Wolffarth agreed, and the maneuver worked. And John Baker had become a runner.

Surge of Energy. The first meet that year (it was 1960) was a 1.7-mile cross-country race through the foothills east of Albuquerque. Most eyes were focused on Albuquerque's reigning state cross-country champion, Lloyd Goff. Immediately after the crack of the gun, the field lined up as expected, with Goff setting the pace and Haaland on his heels. At the end of four minutes, the runners disappeared one by one behind a low hill inside the far turn of the course. A minute passed. Two. Then a lone figure appeared. Coach Wolffarth nudged an assistant. "Here comes Goff," he said. Then he raised his binoculars. "Good grief!" he yelled. "That's not Goff! It's Baker!"

Leaving a field of startled runners far behind, Baker crossed the finish line alone. His time—8:03.5—set a new meet record.

What had happened on the far side of the hill? Baker later explained. Halfway through the race, running well back of the leaders, he had asked himself a question: am I doing my best? He didn't know. Fixing his eye on the back of the runner immediately in front of him, he closed his mind to all else. Only one thing mattered: catch and pass that runner, then go after the next one. An unknown reserve of energy surged through his body. "It was almost hypnotic," Baker recalled. One by one he passed the other runners. Ignoring the fatigue that tore at his muscles, he maintained his furious pace until he crossed the finish line and collapsed in exhaustion.

Had the race been a fluke? As the season progressed, Wolffarth entered Baker in a number of other events, and always the result was the same. Once on the track, the modest, fun-loving teen-ager became a fierce, unrelenting competitor—a "heart" runner who simply wouldn't be beat. By the end of his junior year Baker had broken six state track records, and during his senior year he was proclaimed the finest miler ever developed in the state. He was not yet 18.

"Upset John." In the fall of 1962, Baker entered the University of New Mexico in Albuquerque, and stepped up his training. Each morning at dawn, spray can in hand to ward off snapping dogs, he ran through city streets, parks and golf courses—25 miles a day. All in addition to daily varsity workouts. The training told. Soon, in Abilene, Tulsa, Salt Lake City, wherever the New Mexico Lobos competed, "Upset John" Baker was confounding forecasters by picking off favored runners.

In the spring of 1965, when Baker was a junior, the most feared track team in the nation belonged to the University of Southern California. So when the mighty Trojans descended on Albuquerque for a dual meet, sportscasters predicted doom for the Lobos. The mile, they said, would fall to U.S.C.'s "Big Three"—Chris Johnson, Doug Calhoun and Bruce Bess, in that order. All had better times for the mile than Baker.

Baker led for one lap, then eased purposely back to fourth position. Rattled, Calhoun and Bess moved uneasily into the forfeited lead. Johnson, wary, held back. In the far turn of the third lap, at the same moment, Baker and Johnson moved for the lead—and collided. Fighting to stay on his feet, Baker lost precious yards, and Johnson moved into the lead. With 330 yards to go, Baker kicked into his final sprint. First Bess, then Calhoun, fell back. On the final turn it was Johnson and Baker neck and neck. Slowly, Baker inched ahead. With both hands above his head in a V-for-Victory sign, he broke the tape—a winner by three seconds. Inspired by Baker's triumph, the Lobos swept every following event, handing the demoralized Trojans their third-worst defeat in 65 years.

A Coach Who Cared. Upon graduation, Baker considered his options. There were college coaching offers, but he had always planned to work with children. There was also his running. Was he, he wondered, Olympic material? In the end, he accepted a job that would allow him to pursue both ambitions—he became a coach at Aspen Elementary School in Albuquerque, and at the same time renewed his rigorous training with an eye to the 1972 Games.

At Aspen, another facet of Baker's character emerged. On his playing fields there were no stars, and no criticism for lack of ability. His only demand was that each child do his or her best. This fairness, plus an obviously sincere concern for his students' welfare, triggered a powerful response. Youthful grievances were brought first to Coach Baker. Real or fancied, each was treated as if at the moment it was the most important matter in the world. And the word spread: "Coach cares."

Early in May 1969, shortly before his 25th birthday, Baker noticed that he was tiring prematurely during workouts. Two weeks later, he developed chest pains, and one morning near the end of the month he awoke with painfully swollen groin. He made an appointment to see a doctor.

To urologist Edward Johnson, Baker's symptoms were ominous, requiring immediate exploratory surgery. The operation confirmed Johnson's fears. A cell in one of Baker's testicles had suddenly erupted in cancerous growth, and the mass was already widespread. Though Dr. Johnson didn't say it, he estimated that even with a second operation Baker had approximately six months to live.

At home recuperating for the second operation, Baker confronted the grim reality of his world. There would be no more running, and no Olympics. Almost certainly, his coaching career was ended. Worst of all, his family faced months of anguish.

Edge of the Precipice. On the Sunday before the second operation, Baker left home alone for a drive in the mountains. He was gone for hours. When he returned that evening, there was a marked change in his spirits. His habitual smile, of late only a mask, was again natural and sincere. What's more, for the first time in two weeks he spoke of future plans. Late that night, he told his sister, Jill, what had happened that clear June day.

He had driven to Sandia Crest, the majestic two-mile-high mountain peak that dominates Albuquerque's eastern skyline. Seated in his car near the edge of the precipice, he thought of the extended agony his condition would cause his family. He could end that agony, and his own, in an instant. With a silent prayer, he revved the engine and reached for the emergency brake. Suddenly a vision flashed before his eyes: the faces of the children at Aspen Elementary—the children he had taught to do their best despite the odds. What sort of legacy would his suicide be for them? Shamed to the depths of his soul, he switched off the ignition, slumped in the seat and wept. After a while he realized that his fears were stilled, that he was at peace. "Whatever time I have left," he told himself, "I'm dedicating to the kids."

In September, following extensive abdominal surgery and

a summer of cobalt treatments, Baker reimmersed himself in his job. And to his already full schedule, he added a new commitment—sports for the handicapped. Whatever their infirmity, children who had once stood idle on the sidelines now assumed positions as "Coach's timekeeper" or "chief equipment watcher" or "foul-line supervisor," all wearing their official Aspen jerseys, all eligible to earn a "Coach Baker ribbon" for trying hard. (Baker made the ribbons himself, at home in the evening, from material purchased with his own money.)

Silent Suffering. By Thanksgiving, letters in praise of Baker from grateful parents were arriving almost daily at Aspen (more than 500 would be received there and at the Baker residence before a year had passed). "My son was a morning monster," one mother wrote. "Getting him up, fed and out the door was hardly bearable. Now he can't wait for school. He's the Chief Infield-Raker!"

"Despite my son's assertions, I could not believe that there was a superman at Aspen," wrote another mother. "I drove over secretly to watch Coach Baker with the children. My son was right." And this from two grandparents: "In other schools, our granddaughter suffered terribly from her awkwardness. Then, this wonderful year at Aspen, Coach Baker gave her an 'A' for trying her best. God bless this young man who gave a timid child self-respect."

In December, during a routine visit to Dr. Johnson, Baker complained of a sore throat and headaches. Tests confirmed that the malignancy had spread to his neck and brain. For four months, Johnson now recognized, Baker had been suffering severe pain in silence, using his incredible power of concentration to ignore the pain just as he had used it to ignore fatigue when he ran. Johnson suggested painkilling injections. Baker shook his head. "I want to work with the kids as long as I'm able," he said. "The injections would dull my responsiveness."

"From that moment," Johnson later remarked, "I looked upon John Baker as one of the most unselfish persons I've ever known."

Cups for Dashers. Early in 1970, Baker was asked to help coach a small Albuquerque track club for girls from elementary through high-school age. Its name: the Duke City Dashers. He agreed on the spot and, like the children of Aspen, the girls on the Dashers responded to the new coach with enthusiasm.

One day Baker arrived at a practice session carrying a shoebox. He announced that it held two awards: one for the fleetest runner; and one for the girl who, though never a winner, wouldn't quit. When Baker opened the box, the girls gasped. Inside were two shiny gold trophy cups. From then on, deserving Dashers received such cups. Months later, Baker's family would discover that the trophies were his, from his racing days, with his own name carefully burnished away.

By summer, the Duke City Dashers were a club to contend with, breaking record after record at meets throughout New Mexico and bordering states. Proudly, Baker made a bold prediction: "The Dashers are going to the national AAU finals." (The AAU is the American Athletic Union.)

But now a new problem plagued Baker. His cobalt treatments and frequent chemotherapy injections brought on severe nausea, and he could not keep food down. Despite steadily decreasing stamina, however, he continued to supervise the Dashers, usually sitting on a small hill above the training area, hollering encouragement.

One afternoon in October, following a huddle on the track below, one of the girls ran up the hill toward Baker. "Hey, Coach!" she shouted. "Your prediction's come true! We're invited to the AAU finals in St. Louis next month!"

Elated, Baker confided to friends that he had one remaining hope—to live long enough to go along.

Walking Tall. But it was not to be. On the morning of October 28, at Aspen, Baker suddenly clutched his abdomen and collapsed on the playground. Examination revealed that the spreading tumor had ruptured, triggering shock. Declining hospitalization, Baker insisted on returning to school for one last day. He told his parents that he wanted the children to remember his walking tall, not lying helpless in the dirt.

Sustained now by massive blood transfusions and sedation, Baker realized that for him the St. Louis trip was impossible. So he began telephoning Dashers every evening, and didn't stop until he had urged each girl to do her best at the finals.

In the early evening of November 23, Baker collapsed again. Barely conscious as attendants loaded him into an ambulance, he whispered to his parents, "Make sure the lights are flashing. I want to leave the neighborhood in style." Shortly after dawn on November 26, he turned on his hospital bed to his mother, who was holding his hand, and said, "I'm sorry to have been so much trouble." With a final sigh, he closed his eyes. It was Thanksgiving Day of 1970, 18 months after John Baker's first visit to Dr. Johnson. He had beaten the odds against death by 12 months.

Two days later, with tears streaming down their cheeks, the Duke City Dashers won the AAU championship in St. Louis— "for Coach Baker."

That would be the end of the John Baker story except for a phenomenon which occurred after his funeral. A few of the children of Aspen began calling their school "John Baker School," and the change of name spread like wildfire. Then a movement began to make the new name official. "It's *our* school," the kids said, "and we want to call it 'John Baker.'" Aspen officials referred the matter to the Albuquerque school board, and the board suggested a voter referendum. In early spring of 1971, 520 families in the Aspen district voted on the question. There were 520 votes for; none against.

That May, in a ceremony attended by hundreds of Baker's friends and all of "his" children, Aspen School officially became John Baker Elementary. It stands today as a visible monument to a courageous young man who, in his darkest hours, transformed bitter tragedy into an enduring legacy.

A Champion Tenor Defends His Title

by William H. Honan

Just moments before the orchestra commenced the prelude to Mascagni's *Cavalleria Rusticana* on January 8, 1970, Franco Corelli, an Italian tenor, took his place backstage at the New York Metropolitan Opera trembling with fear. His pulse, normally a lethargic 58, was throbbing at 130. His teeth chattered, his legs were quivering like mandolin strings, and he glanced about wildly as if seeking to escape.

Corelli was then generally acknowledged to possess the most titanic human noise-making machine since Enrico Caruso. But all such machinery, Corelli knew only too well, is fragile and balky. "You can start superbly," he explained in Italian, "but who knows what will happen after five minutes? The throat may close! Or the voice may go completely dead! It has happened to me."

To add to Corelli's worries, this performance was of unusual importance. It was the event at which, in effect, the world's champion tenor had been called upon to defend his title. Because of a musicians' strike following the summer hiatus, Corelli had not performed an opera for almost seven months. Moreover, he had cancelled a whole slew of performances the previous season in order to be in Italy. In his absence, general manager Rudolf Bing had relied on Spanish tenor Placido Domingo for roles Corelli would normally have sung. Now Corelli was hard pressed to re-establish himself.

Not the least among this fears was the veritable Chinese torture that composer Mascagni had devised for the tenor at the opening of the opera—the aria known (and dreaded) by tenors around the world as "Siciliana." Relatively short and excruciatingly high, it obliges the tenor to scream at the top of his lungs for two minutes, from offstage. Worse, "Siciliana" is the first voice heard by the audience, and the tenor is thus afforded no warm-up, no chance to test the house and build up his confidence. He has to go off like a cannon. Many tenors find "Siciliana" so impossible to sing well that they race through it, on the theory that the less time they are exposed at a disadvantage, the better.

But great conductor Leonard Bernstein asked that it be sung particularly slowly. It must be sung *"s-o-s-t-e-n-u-t-o,"* he kept telling Corelli, which meant that the agony was to be prolonged, the big voice tested to its limit. "Corelli can handle it," Bernstein remarked with a chuckle. "He's got the lungs of a camel." The result, in rehearsal, had been the slowest— and one of the most hauntingly beautiful— "Sicilianas" in memory. But Corelli had sung it half-voice. Could he in performance burst forth with it in full voice, and at this agonizing tempo?

Leonine Capacity. Franco Corelli at the time was a tall (six feet, two inches), strikingly good-looking 41-year-old with wide, brown, lady-killing eyes. Some fans admired his legs as much as his voice. He is one of the very few genuinely "tall, dark and handsome" tenors in opera. (No one knows why, but tenors generally run short, squat and ugly.)

He is well-built from a musical standpoint, too. He has a capacious mouth and the lungs of, if not a camel, at least a glassblower. At rest, his chest measurement is 47 inches. In two seconds he can inhale almost 300 cubic inches (four and a half quarts) of air, and then his chest measures 50 inches. These endowments give him the leonine capacity to outshout all the woodwinds and trumpets of a 90-piece symphony orchestra and flood the opera house with rafter-shaking sound. And when he feels like it he can hold a high note, as critic Harold Schonberg once put it, until the baritone needs a shave. On the "Ed Sullivan Show" once he hit a B-flat at the end of a long phrase and let it rip for 17 gooseflesh-producing seconds.

Corelli is endowed with plenty of temperament, too. Once, while singing *Il Trovatore* in Naples, he was booed by a student. Corelli raced backstage, bolted up three flights of stairs, broke down the door to the young man's box, and when finally restrained, had his stage sword half drawn.

There is another story heard backstage at the Met (although Corelli denies it) that one evening when he was supposed to give soprano Birgit Nilsson a stage kiss, he bit her on the neck instead—because she had hung on to the high C in a duet longer than he did. Next day, Nilsson is alleged to have wired general manager Bing: "I cannot go to Cleveland. Have rabies."

Ritualistic Agony. The day Corelli was to sing *Cavalleria Rusticana,* he dragged himself out of bed at 3 p.m. He had spent half the night pacing and fitfully watching TV. Brunch consisted of a glass of two-thirds tea and one-third honey—a throat relaxer—and he avoided using his voice even to talk. After calisthenics and a walk, he dined in silence with his wife, Loretta, a pert blonde. Dinner was his standard pre-performance fare—a little less than a pound of steak *tartare* garnished with three or four lemons, oil and quantities of garlic. (The after-effects of the garlic, says Corelli with a smile, have caused more than one soprano to lose her footing when he projected his voice at her.)

At six o'clock, Corelli began singing exercises and snatches from the role he was about to perform. He was getting terrifically keyed up. As he dressed for the opera house, he could feel his heart beginning to pound. By the time he darted out of his apartment, opera-bound, his lips pursed tightly to protect his throat from the biting air, he was a tortured wretch.

Three minutes before curtain, Stanley Levine, the Met stage manager, tapped on Corelli's dressing-room door. Inside, Corelli was fervently praying. And then, in ritualistic emotional agony, the world's most famous operatic tenor asked himself: "Do you think you can sing this opera tonight?" His answer was: "When I am alone, it is very easy. But now? Before this audience? No, *I can't do it!*"

Levine knocked on the door again. Corelli snapped on his portable tape recorder beside the house intercom (he records and later analyzes all of his performances) and emerged, casting Levine a gloomy look. Like a warden with his prisoner reluctantly shuffling behind, Levine led Corelli down a staircase to a concealed hollow beneath the stage. Here several people were huddled around a gold concert harp, a harmonium (which resembles an upright piano and is used for giving singers the exact pitch) and a small TV screen on which Maestro Bernstein could be viewed taking his bow. The applause for Bernstein from the nearly 4000 people on the other side of the curtain sounded like a distant waterfall.

"No voice. No voice," Corelli whispered, pointing to his throat. "Oh, well," Levine replied, having heard this routine before, "you'll just have to sing it half-voice, Franco."

Below stage, as the applause following the prelude and the raising of the curtain died away, associate conductor Ignace Strasfogel gave a couple of beats with his left hand and then motioned to the harpist, who produced a few exquisitely watery ripples. Then Strasfogel pointed to Corelli. Corelli, with one foot forward and chest thrown out, opened his mouth wide—and out swam a gargantuan and voluptuous wail: *"O Lo-la . . ."*

Daringly high, the notes were shortly followed by other bars, higher yet, which Corelli belted out with an even more mighty burst. As he continued, he sank into a crouch and writhed torturously. His heart was palpitating so wildly that his head began to spin, and he clutched the harmonium for support. He concluded with the difficult *pianissimo,* meant to suggest that his voice was fading off into the distance. Then he collapsed over the top of the harmonium. There was an instant roar from the house. Yet the audience was unable to witness what was surely the most dramatic spectacle of the entire performance—Corelli sprawled across the harmonium, rolling his head from side to side and gasping for breath like a fainting marathon runner.

It was not all his histrionics. Corelli had strained, and he knew it. Slowly, he raised himself from the harmonium and lumbered off. As he ascended the staircase, he muttered, "*Sostenuto. Sosten-u-u-u-to!*" and growled in self-reproach. When he appeared in the wings, several other singers waiting for their cues greeted him with "Bravo, Franco," "*Magnifico,*" "Nice going." Groaning and acting as if he had been pelted with tomatoes rather than enthusiastic applause, he returned to his dressing room and banged the door shut—feeling "miserable," as he recalled later. He had a 20-minute wait.

A Force of Nature. *Cavalleria Rusticana* ("Rustic Chivalry") is a short firecracker of an opera about a handsome and cocky young Sicilian named Turiddu, who plays around with a couple of local belles and winds up getting his throat cut in a knife fight with a husband.

Corelli likes Turiddu; they have things in common. Corelli, too, grew up in a small Italian town. The son of a naval engineer, with no particular interest in music, he was a first-year engineering student at the University of Bologna when a friend entered his name in a singing contest as a joke. Surprisingly, he won—and dropped out of school to study singing. Still more surprisingly, conservatory lessons caused him to lose his voice.

Thereafter, Corelli taught himself, listening by the hour to the records of Caruso and other great tenors. Though some critics may detect in Corelli an imperfect musicianship, to most opera-goers this is not all-important. For opera is not fundamentally a "listening experience"; it is a dramatic experience. Going to the opera is like going to a hurricane: one should expect to be assailed by a gigantic and unruly force of nature. And that is what the Franco Corelli experience is all about.

Shimmering A-Flat. Levine tapped on his door again: "Franco? Ready, Fran-co?" Corelli came out, taking slurps of tea and honey from a paper cup. A few minutes later, he bounded on stage for his big scene with mezzo-soprano Grace Bumbry and contralto Nedda Casei. This time it was a piece of cake. The music was direct, lushly melodic and animated by unabashed vigor. Corelli sang with seeming effortlessness and to stunning effect, and at the end of the scene the audience went wild with applause.

At the end comes *Addio alla madre,* the spectacular final

aria, in which Turiddu says good-by to his mother just before rushing off to the fatal duel. Corelli did not tiptoe up to the aria; he swaggered to it. His first cry of "Mamma!" had the solidity of a church bell; yet it was exciting, too, because of a tinge of anxiety. Then, suddenly, as Turiddu blurts out that he does not expect to return and implores Mamma Lucia to "be a mother" to the girl he has made pregnant, Corelli's voice exploded in melodic sobs and gasps mingled with shimmering, golden A's, A-flats and B-flats. They were the cries of a stricken animal, not in the least ethereal but virile and garlicky. The last of the notes—a ravishing A-flat—soared through the opera house like a great bird released from the stage.

This time the audience went berserk. Voices quaking with emotion shouted "Bra-a-a-vo!" and there were shrieks and whistles. As Corelli came pounding offstage, he, too, seemed a little deranged. An assistant stage manager hustled him back onstage to take his curtain calls. There were six of them. Each time the applause grew into a roar. Gradually, a broad, sparkling smile took possession of Corelli's face, and by the time he returned to the wings he was jubilant.

His exertions in the past hour and 20 minutes had wrung from his body nearly three pounds. Physically and emotionally spent, Corelli would need several 10- or 12-hour nights of sleep to recover. But now, striding back to his dressing room, he was asking himself once more, "Do you think you can sing this opera tonight?" The answer was: "*Si! Si!* I *did* sing this opera tonight!"

Man
of the Family

My Father's Hands

by Calvin R. Worthington

His hands were rough and exceedingly strong. He could gently prune a fruit tree or firmly wrestle an ornery mule into harness. He could draw a square with quick accuracy. He had been known to peel his knuckles upside a tough jaw. But what I remember most is the special warmth from those hands soaking through my shirt as he would take me by the shoulder and, hunkering down beside my ear, point out the glittering swoop of a blue hawk, or a rabbit asleep in its lair. They were good hands that served him well and failed him in only one thing: they never learned to write.

My father was illiterate. The number of illiterates in our country has steadily declined, but if there were only one I would be saddened, remembering my father and the pain he endured because his hands never learned to write.

He started in the first grade, where the remedy for a wrong answer was ten ruler strokes across a stretched palm. For some reason, shapes, figures and recitations just didn't fall into the right pattern inside his six-year-old towhead. Maybe he suffered from some type of learning handicap such as dyslexia. His father took him out of school after several months and set him to a man's job on the farm.

Years later, his wife, with her fourth-grade education, would try to teach him to read. And still later I would grasp his big fist between my small hands and awkwardly help him trace the letters of his name. He submitted to the ordeal, but soon grew restless. Flexing his fingers and kneading his palms, he would declare that he had had enough and depart for a long, solitary walk.

Finally, one night when he thought no one saw, he slipped away with his son's second-grade reader and labored over the words, until they became too difficult. He pressed his forehead into the pages and wept. "Jesus—Jesus—not even a child's book?" Thereafter, no amount of persuading could bring him to sit with pen and paper.

From the farm to road building and later factory work, his hands served him well. His mind was keen, his will to work unsurpassed. During World War II, he was a pipefitter in a shipyard and installed the complicated guts of mighty fighting ships. His enthusiasm and efficiency brought an offer to become line boss—until he was handed the qualification test. His fingers could trace a path across the blueprints while his mind imagined the pipes lacing through the heart of the ship. He could recall every twist and turn of the pipes. But he couldn't read or write.

After the shipyard closed, he went to the cotton mill, where he labored at night, and stole from his sleeping hours the time required to run the farm. When the mill shut down, he went out each morning looking for work—only to return night after night and say to Mother as she fixed his dinner, "They just don't want anybody who can't take their tests."

It had always been hard for him to stand before a man and make an X mark for his name, but the hardest moment of all was when he placed "his mark" by the name someone else had written for him, and saw another man walk away with the deed to his beloved farm. When it was over, he stood before the window and slowly turned the pen he still held in his hands—gazing, unseeing, down the mountainside. I went to the springhouse that afternoon and wept for a long while.

Eventually, he found another cotton-mill job, and we moved into a millhouse village with a hundred look-alike houses. He never quite adjusted to town life. The blue of his eyes faded; the skin across his cheekbones became a little slack. But his hands kept their strength, and their warmth still soaked through when he would sit me on his lap and ask that I read to him from the Bible. He took great pride in my reading and would listen for hours as I struggled through the awkward phrases.

Once he had heard "a radio preacher" relate that the Bible said, "The man that doesn't provide for his family is worse than a thief and an infidel and will never enter the Kingdom of Heaven." Often he would ask me to read that part to him, but I was never able to find it. Other times, he would sit at the kitchen table leafing through the pages as though by a miracle he might be able to read the passage should he turn to the right page. Then he would sit staring at the Book, and I knew he was wondering if God was going to refuse him entry into heaven because his hands couldn't write.

When Mother left once for a weekend to visit her sister, Dad went to the store and returned with food for dinner while I was busy building my latest homemade wagon. After the meal he said he had a surprise for dessert, and went out to the kitchen, where I could hear him opening a can. Then everything was quiet. I went to the doorway, and saw him standing before the sink with an open can in his hand. "The picture looked just like pears," he mumbled. He walked out and sat on the back steps, and I knew he had been embarrassed before his son. The can read "Whole White Potatoes," but the picture on the label did look a great deal like pears.

I went and sat beside him, and asked if he would point out the stars. He knew where the Big Dipper and all the other stars were located, and we talked about how they got there in the first place. He kept that can on a shelf in the woodshed for a long while, and a few times I saw him turning it in his hands as if the touch of the words would teach his hands to write.

Years later, when Mom died, I tried to get him to come live with my family, but he insisted on staying in his small frame house on the edge of town with a few farm animals and a garden plot. His health was failing, and he was in and out of the hospital with several mild heart attacks. Old Doc Green saw him weekly and gave him medication, including nitroglycerin tablets to put under his tongue should he feel an attack coming on.

My last fond memory of Dad was watching as he walked across the brow of a hillside meadow, with those big, warm hands—now gnarled with age—resting on the shoulders of my two children. He stopped to point out, confidentially, a pond where he and I had swum and fished years before. That night, my family and I flew to a new job and new home, overseas. Three weeks later, he was dead of a heart attack.

I returned alone for the funeral. Doc Green told me how sorry he was. In fact, he was bothered a bit, because he had just written Dad a new nitroglycerin prescription, and the druggist had filled it. Yet the bottle of pills had not been found on Dad's person. Doc Green felt that a pill might have kept him alive long enough to summon help.

An hour before the chapel service, I found myself standing near the edge of Dad's garden, where a neighbor had found him. In grief, I stopped to trace my fingers in the earth where a great man had reached the end of life. My hand came to rest on a half-buried brick, which I aimlessly lifted and tossed aside, before noticing underneath it the twisted and battered, yet unbroken, soft plastic bottle that had been beaten into the soft earth.

As I held the bottle of nitroglycerin pills, the scene of Dad struggling to remove the cap and in desperation trying to break the bottle with the brick flashed painfully before my eyes. With deep anguish I knew why those big warm hands had lost in their struggle with death. For there, imprinted on the bottle cap, were the words, "Child-Proof Cap—Push Down and Twist to Unlock." The druggist later confirmed that he had just started using the new safety bottle.

I knew it was not a purely rational act, but I went right downtown and bought a leather-bound pocket dictionary and a gold pen set. I bade Dad good-by by placing them in those big old hands, once so warm, which had lived so well, but had never learned to write.

God and My Father

by Clarence Day

The religious ideas of my strong-minded, conservative father were straightforward and simple. From boyhood he accepted churches as a natural part of his surroundings. He would never have invented such things himself. But they were here and he regarded them as unquestioningly as he did banks. They were substantial structures, respectable, decent, and frequented by the right sort of people.

On the other hand he never allowed churches—or banks—to dictate to him. He gave each the respect due it, from his point of view; but he also expected from each the respect he felt due to him. Above all, the one thing a church should not tamper with was a man's soul. Such intrusion was distinctly ungentlemanly—after all a man's soul was his own personal affair. And when our rector talked of imitating the saints, it seemed drivel to Father. Father regarded himself as a more all-round man than the saints. From his point of view they had neglected nine-tenths of their duties—they had no business connections, no families, they hadn't even paid taxes.

My mother, who more than made up for the piety Father lacked, once wrote in my plush-covered autograph album, "Fear God and keep his commandments": but the motto that Father wrote was, "Do your duty and fear no one." Father's code was definite and undisputable. It was to be upright, fearless and honorable, and to brush your clothes properly; and in general always to do the right thing in every department of life. The right thing to do for religion was to go to some good church on Sundays.

Father never doubted the existence of God. On the contrary, God and Father had somehow achieved a strange but harmonious relationship. He seemed to envisage a God in his own image—a God who had small use for emotionalism and who prized strength and dignity, although he could never understand why God had peopled the world with "so many damn fools and Democrats." God and Father seldom met: their spheres were so different; but they had perfect confidence in each other and, Father thought, saw eye to eye in most things.

For example, God must feel most affectionately toward my mother, just as he did. God knew she had faults, but He saw she was lovely and good—despite some mistaken ideas she had about money. Naturally God loved Mother, as everyone must. At the gate of Heaven, if there was any misunderstanding about his own ticket, Father counted on Mother to get him in. That was her affair.

Unlike Mother, Father never had any moments of feeling "unworthy." This was a puzzle to Mother. Other people went to church to be made better, she told him. Why didn't he? He replied in astonishment that he had no need to be better—he was all right as he was. It wasn't at all easy for Father to see that he had any faults; and if he did, it didn't even occur to him to ask God to forgive them. He forgave them himself. In his moments of prayer, when he and God tried to commune with each other, it wasn't his own shortcomings that were brought on the carpet, but God's.

Father expected a good deal of God. Not that he wanted God's help; far less His guidance. But God—like the rest of us—sometimes spoiled Father's plans. Father was always trying to bring some good thing to pass, only to meet with obstacles. Wrathfully he would call God's attention to them. He didn't actually accuse God of inefficiency, but when he prayed his tone was loud and angry, like that of a dissatisfied guest in a carelessly managed hotel.

I never saw Father kneel in supplication. He usually talked with God lying in bed. On those nights the sound of damns would float up to my room—at first tragic and low, then loud and exasperated. At the peak of these, I would hear him call "Oh, God?" over and over, with a rising inflection, as though he were demanding that God should present himself instantly, and sit in the fat green chair in the corner to be duly admonished. Then when Father felt that God was listening, he would recite his current botheration and begin to expostulate in a discouraged but strong voice, "Oh, God, it's too much. Amen. . . . I say it's too damned much. . . . No, no, I can't stand it. Amen." After a pause, if he didn't feel better, he would suspect that God might be trying to sneak back to Heaven without doing anything, and I would hear him shout warningly, "Oh, God! I *won't* stand it! A-a-men." Sometimes he would ferociously bark a few extra Amens, and then, soothed and satisfied, peacefully go to sleep.

Father's behavior in church was often a source of sorrow to Mother. He usually started at peace with the world, settled contentedly in his end seat. The Episcopal service in general he didn't criticize—it was stately and quiet, but the sermon was always a gamble. If bad, his expression would darken as he struggled to control himself. At such times Mother, who had been anxiously watching him out of the corner of her eye, would say, "Clare, you mustn't." To which Father would reply, "Bah!"

One day a visiting rector went too far. Ending his sermon he drew a fanciful picture of a businessman at the close of his day. He described how this hard-headed man sat surrounded by ledgers, and how after studying them for hours he chanced to look out of his window at the light in God's sky, and then it came to him that money and ledgers were dross. Whereat, as twilight spread over the city, this strange businessman bowed his head, and with streaming eyes resolved to devote his life to Far Higher Things.

"Oh, damn," Father burst out, so explosively that the man

across the aisle jumped, and I heard old Mrs. Tillotson, in the second pew behind, titter.

Aside from the untruth of such a picture of business, to Father the whole attitude was pernicious. Anyone dreamy enough to think of money as "dross" was bound to get in hot water.

When hymns were sung Father usually stood silent as the eagle among doves, leaving others to abase themselves in sentiments he didn't share.

> Cover my defenseless head
> With the shadow of thy wing.

How could Father sing that? His head was far from defenseless, and he would have scorned to ask shelter. As he stood there, high-spirited, resolute, I could imagine him marching with that same independence through space—a tiny speck masterfully dealing with death and infinity.

It was Father's custom to put one dollar in the contribution plate weekly. It bothered Mother dreadfully to see Father give so little. Father's reply was that a dollar was a good, handsome sum, and that it would be better for Mother if she could learn this. He had a great deal to say on this point. But after a while Mother made him feel it was beneath his dignity not to give more. Even then he didn't surrender; he compromised instead: before starting for church he put his usual dollar in his right-hand waistcoat pocket, but in the lefthand pocket he put a new five-dollar bill; and he stated that from now on he would make a handsome offer: let the rector preach a decent sermon and he would give him the five.

When the rector entered the pulpit we boys watched with a thrill, as though he were a racehorse at the barrier. He usually either robbed himself of the prize in the very first lap by getting off on the wrong foot—or after a blameless beginning, he would run clear off the course that Father had in silence marked out for him, and gallop away unconsciously in some other direction. It gave a boy a sobering sense of the grimness of fate.

One day the rector began talking about the need for what he called a New Edifice. Father paid little attention to this until he realized that he, too, would have to subscribe. Then he became roused. He said he might have known it was just a damn scheme to get money.

He was still more upset when Mother said that, since he had a good pew, they would expect him to give a big sum. This was like an earthquake. Father barricaded himself every evening in the library and declared he wouldn't see any callers. Later, however, when he had cooled down a bit, Mother told him he'd at least have to see the committee.

He waited, fretful and uneasy. One night Mother heard sounds in the library. Father was doing all the talking, stating his sentiments in his usual strong, round tones. He got more and more shouty. Mother began to fear the committee mightn't like being scolded. But when she peeked in, there was no one there but Father, thumping his hand with a hammerlike beat on his newspaper. "In ordinary circumstances," he was saying to the imaginary committeemen, "I should have expected to subscribe to this project. But recently my investments" (thump, thump, on the newspaper) "have shown me heavy losses." Here he thought of the New Haven Railroad and groaned. "*Damned* heavy losses!" he roared. "Who the devil's that? Oh, it's you, Vinnie. Come in, dear Vinnie. I'm lonely."

In the end he gave literally—as befitted his status in the church. Our pew had cost Father $5000, and though he hated to invest all that money in a mere place to sit, he could sell out again some day. Pews were like seats on the stock exchange, fluctuating in price as demand rose or fell. Father used to ask Mother periodically for the current quotation. When she came home with the news that the last sale had been for $3200, Father said she had led him into this against his better judgment, and now the bottom was dropping out of the market. He swore if that damn pew ever went up again he would unload it on somebody.

When Mother married Father she had naturally supposed him a good churchman. But one day she chanced to find out from Grandpa that Father had never been baptized. I doubt if I can even imagine what a shock this was to my devout mother. She hurried home with her terrible news, supposing that as soon as Father heard it he would be baptized at once. But he flatly refused.

"If you won't be baptized," Mother wailed, "you aren't a Christian at all."

"Why, confound it, of course I'm a Christian," Father roundly declared. "A damned good Christian, too. A lot better Christian than those psalm-singing donkeys at church!"

Father's general position seemed to be that he didn't object to baptism. It was all right for savages, for instance. But among civilized people it should come only when one was young.

For months Mother waged an unsuccessful campaign to get Father baptized. Then at long last it seemed she might prevail. She had a bad illness, which worried Father so much that when she kept begging him to do this thing for her he said he would. But when she was well again he said flatly he had no recollection of having agreed to it, probably her fever had made her misunderstand him.

Mother kept telling him she simply couldn't believe he would go back on his Sacred Promise—as she began calling it. Father was unperturbed. Downtown, his lightest word to anybody was binding, of course, but that was in the real world of business. Getting baptized was all poppycock.

Finally, under Mother's constant attacks Father went into the whole matter as thoroughly as a railroad report. He asked just how wet would a man have to get. Exactly what rigmarole would he have to go through? He said if it wasn't too complicated, perhaps he'd consider it, just to please her.

He was startled to learn that he couldn't have an accommodating parson baptize him quietly some morning at the house, after breakfast; no, the performance would have to take place in a church; and, worse, there would have to be others present. Father declared he certainly wasn't going to be made a fool of in that way.

At last Mother discovered a distant parish set in thick, quiet woods. She thought this would suit Father, since he seemed bent on "confessing God before men" only when no one was looking. Mr. Morley, the rector, agreed to make everything as easy for Father as possible.

Father agreed, and the great day arrived. He came down to breakfast in a good temper that morning, and the bacon and eggs suited him for once. Mother gave a happy, tender look at this soul she was saving. The dining room seemed full of sunshine, and the whole world light-hearted. But when Mother said the cab was waiting, Father demanded what cab. He listened to her answer in horror and sprang up with a roar.

It was as though an elephant which had been tied up with infinite pains had trumpeted and burst every fetter. Mother stood up to him, armed with God's word and also, as she despairingly reminded him, with his own Sacred Promise. When these arguments failed, Mother fell back on her last weapon: the waiting cab. Wasting money on cabs was simply unheard of in our family. When we ordered a cab we did not keep it waiting. This cab, now at the door, reached those depths of Father's spirit which God couldn't.

As we drove out of the city, Father's wrath became increasingly bitter. Apparently he had confidentially believed up to this very moment that Heaven would intervene and spare him this dose.

When we reached the church Father glowered like a bull in the ring, waiting to charge the reverend toreador. He felt hurt, outraged and lonely. His whole private life had been pried into, even his babyhood. He had wished to take his religion aloof, as a gentleman should. Mr. Morley, a shy, earnest man, approached our little group trustingly, to shake Father' hand, but he got such a look he turned to me instead and patted me on the head several times.

When Mr. Morley came to the part in the service: "Dost thou renounce the devil and all his works, the vain pomp and glory of the world?" Father looked as though he might have been an annoyed Roman general, participating much against his will in a low and barbaric rite.

At last the great moment came for the actual baptism. I remember how Father stood, grim and erect, in his tailed morning coat; but when I saw Mr. Morley dip his hand in the water and make a pass at Father's forehead, I shut my eyes tightly at this frightful sacrilege, and whether he actually landed or not I never knew.

When the service was over, we stood awkwardly for a moment. Then Mr. Morley began piously to urge Father to "mortify all his evil affections," but Father broke in, saying abruptly, "I shall be late at the office," and strode down the aisle.

As we drove off, Mother sank back into her corner of the cab, quite worn out. Father was still seething, as though his very soul was boiling over. He got out at the nearest Elevated station, thrust his red face in the cab window, and with a burning look at Mother said, "I hope you are satisfied." Then this new son of the church took out his watch, gave a start, and Mother and I heard him shout "Hell!" as he raced up the stairs.

"HAVE SOME RALLY!"
by Gerald Moore

Cathy burst into the house that fall afternoon and went straight to her room. I could see that my 13-year-old daughter was in the darkest corner of depression, and I tried to think what might have happened at school to send her into this emotional storm. Then I went to see if I could help.

Cathy was face down on her bed, not crying but about to. She told me that she had been defeated in her run for the student council—by seven votes.

"You know, Dad, it really is the only thing I wanted this year," she said. "I wish I hadn't even tried."

"But you ran a good race. You came awfully close."

"It doesn't matter," she shot back. "I lost."

Bothered by her self-pitying tone, I said, "Oh, Cathy, have some rally!"

"You always say that. Grandma, too. I don't even know what 'Have some rally' means."

Suddenly and vividly, I remembered the day when I learned what the phrase meant. I tried to define it precisely for Cathy: "It's having the grace to think of others at the worst moment of your life."

"Then no one has 'rally,'" Cathy said with great confidence.

"Your grandfather did," I replied with equal confidence.

"You saw the worst moment of his life?"

"I think I did. Shall I tell you about it?"

Cathy wrapped her arms around her legs and prepared to listen as I pulled my mind back to a certain autumn Sunday in 1945.

We had been to church—mother, my younger sister, Sharron, and I. Normally Dad would have been with us, but he was shipping calves from the railroad stockyards in Vaughan, a tiny town not far from our New Mexico ranch.

He had been in high spirits when he left us the day before. We had been blessed with the best spring anyone could remember. Rain had come by the inch, and the tough, nutritious grama grass throve in the moist soil. It was the best stand of grass seen in 15 years. For the first time we wouldn't have to buy winter feed for the Hereford cattle Dad so prized, and the money saved would pay debts that had been piling up for nearly a decade.

Dad had started building the ranch in the mid-1920s, soon after he finished high school. But the Depression hit before he had paid for the land. Not being a whiner or a quitter, he simply ducked his head, worked and endured. Through careful management and enormous sacrifices, he was able to keep the place together through the '30s.

I am sure the day he hung the little white sign saying "Moore Ranch—Registered Herefords" at the entrance to the ranch he meant it to be accurate. Reflected there was his dream of fine fat cattle grazing on silken pastures, of freshly painted barns, and of sturdy bull calves that would draw cattlemen from across the state to nod their approval.

Yet the reality was somewhat different. Beyond that sign Dad raised more unregistered than registered cattle. A forbidding, deeply rutted dirt road led to our house. Dad had himself built the house, a small structure made of adobe and plastered but never painted. He controlled 10,000 acres, but half were leased from the state or the Southern Pacific Railroad. We had no electricity, no running water, and no phone until he put in 14 miles of phone line with his own hands.

This particular Sunday we needed that phone. We were driving home from church when Mother leaned forward and stared at the horizon. "Do you see smoke?" she asked us children—and then ordered suddenly, "Hang on!" She hit the accelerator of our old pickup truck and hardly slowed even for the turn across the cattle guard at the entrance to the ranch. Smoke was clearly visible now, staining the sky above the rolling hills.

Near the house we had to go through a wire gate to enter the south pasture. I jumped out to open it. "Leave it open!" Mother shouted. Gates were *never* left open, but I obeyed and scooted back into the truck.

We drove only a mile before we saw it: a wall of pale yellow flames, almost invisible in the bright sunlight. The rising heat made the land seem to shimmer and wobble. The flames were moving toward us before a fall breeze. Off to the east three cows and a heifer calf loped ahead of the fire, their tails up behind them like masts.

Sharron started to cry. Mother's voice came from low in her throat: "Oh, no!" I felt the skin on my arms and back tighten. Mother made a tight circle before the oncoming fire and headed back to the house. I will never forget the sight of her at that moment. There were tears in her brown eyes. Her hands gripped the steering wheel so tightly her knuckles went white. When Sharron bounced and hit her head as the truck leaped over a bump, Mother said in a dead-calm voice, "Gerald, put your sister on the seat *and hold her there.*"

At the house she jumped out and sprinted for the phone.

Neighbors came in twos and threes until there were about 15 families gathered. Most were still in their Sunday clothes. I was eight and not much help, but Mother sent me to the barn to collect feed sacks. The heavy burlap, soaked in water, would be the only weapon against the fire. Vaughan had a two-truck fire department, but the trucks were worthless so far from water.

When Dad arrived from Vaughan, he took charge. He sent Tom Foxx off to the windmill to fill a 500-gallon tank we kept on the back of an ancient truck. That would be enough to keep the sacks wet for a time. The children were herded into the yard and put under the supervision of the oldest Thompson girl.

Through the afternoon, 40 men and women stood shoulder to shoulder in a pitifully short line and beat at the flames with wet sacks. For one dreadful hour it seemed the wind would push the fire toward the house and barn, but by four o'clock it was clear that the fire would burn to the east and spare the buildings.

About nightfall the blaze reached the highway. There that spring, in his customary precise manner, Dad had plowed a wide firebreak in the lush grass to protect the ranch from cigarettes and matches that might be thrown out of passing cars. When the fire reached that bare earth, it hesitated. The bone-weary men and women seized the moment and beat it out.

But half our ranch was a smoldering carpet of black fibers too hot to walk on. Twenty head of cattle, trapped in a fence corner, were charred. Five more were burned so badly Dad had to shoot them. And with the fury of the flames had gone all his hopes of pulling out of debt—all his hopes, really, of having a ranch at all.

Yet he stood in the yard, shaking hands with each neighbor, thanking them all for coming to help. When the last car's taillights disappeared, he came inside. I saw that the new boots he had bought on the promise of the fat calves were ruined.

It would be weeks before the cattle were sorted and fenced. It would be only days before he had to think of buying winter feed. I was looking at a man who had fought hard but lost everything. As he took some coffee from Mother, I watched, feeling all the horror of the day, but fascinated by the lean, haggard man seated at the kitchen table.

Suddenly he reached out, put his arm around my waist and looked directly at me. "Had quite a bonfire, didn't we, boy?"

"Did the cows burn up?" I asked.

"Some."

"You ruined your boots."

He leaned down to inspect what remained of the fine black boots. "Well," he said, "they'll make good work boots, and we're both going to need some."

I wanted to hug him, but I didn't. I wanted to cry, but I

didn't. I offered the only thing I could think of.

"You can have my war bond if you want it," I said.

His face broke into a grin. "You hang onto that bond, boy. You might want to make a trip to Singapore someday."

"Singapore?" I said, unable to fathom what he meant.

"Sure, all young men go to Singapore, didn't you know that? I spent seven years in Singapore before you were born."

"You didn't really."

"Ask your mother," he said, turning to her. "She wouldn't have married anyone who hadn't been to Singapore." Then he laughed, and I saw Mother's face lift. We all laughed—and for a moment forgot about the fire. Mother sat down on his lap and put an arm around his neck and looked at him with pure love.

"Ben," she said, "you have more damn rally than a Roman army."

I don't think I had ever heard the word before, but I knew instantly that it was something worth having.

When I finished my story, Cathy sat thinking for a moment before she spoke. "You know, Dad," she said, "that story makes me feel very proud and very ashamed."

The next fall, Cathy was elected to the student council by a landslide. I promised her—much as I hate to give it up—that if she does a good job I will give her the old, battered white sign that used to hang so proudly at the entrance to the Moore ranch.

He Played
Trombone for Me
by Robert Hohler

It is night now. The hospital sounds of supper carts and evening rounds have subsided. The drugs they have given my father have finally taken hold and he is resting calmly, peacefully. He is dying. A matter of hours, the doctors say. As I sit there beside his bed, half awake and half dreaming, my mind is full of childhood memories.

I am in my mother's steamy kitchen. She is boiling clothes on the stove, and the strong yellow laundry soap fills the room with its acrid smell. She turns toward me, shaking her head. "Bobby, go outside and play. You're going to ruin your eyes with all that reading."

"In a minute, Ma." The fact is I have not been reading at all. I have been sitting at the kitchen table pretending to read, while I wait for my father. I've heard him stirring in the bedroom, and I know it will soon be time for him to go to work.

I slip from the kitchen into the living room. After a while I hear him talking to my mother. They are having words, as usual. He has come home late again. Finally, I hear a chair being pushed back from the kitchen table, and I sense his presence in the doorway. He is standing there, smiling. His shoulders are slightly stooped; he is bald.

"Are you going to work now?" I ask.

"In a while. I'm going to practice first."

This is what I had waited for. He goes to the hall closet, brings back a black-leather case and opens it to expose the gleaming gold and silver parts of a trombone.

He pieces the instrument together, manipulating the slide up and down, testing it for freeness and fluidity, dropping oil along its length, carefully wiping it. Then, finally, the room full of the delicious smell of oil and leather, he inserts the mouthpiece and begins softly to play.

He stands before me, eyes closed, body swaying, encircling me in liquid notes and sending me afloat to a world that only he and I share.

I loved these moments. And I loved my father.

He made his living playing the big-band swing music of the 1930s. He could and did play classical music. But his first love was jazz, and his idols were Bix Beiderbecke, Jack Teagarden, Louis Armstrong, Bunny Berigan. Music began after the night's gig was over and the saccharin-sweet swing arrangements were put away. Then he and his fellow musicians were free to create, improvise, experiment—playing music that was not written down anywhere. Jazz. It was his love. It was also to be his undoing.

My father showed musical promise very early, and his German father saw to it he had the best teacher in town, a first trombonist in John Philip Sousa's band. At 18, he had earned a berth in a traveling band that played the big ballrooms in the Northeast. Soon he was a veteran of the one-night stands.

To be a steadily employed musician in the early '30s was to be a gypsy. Life centered around a bus, and a big-band bus was "vice on wheels." Drugs, booze, gambling, interleaved with feuding, bickering, fistfights. (One of my early memories is of a drunken brawl between two musicians, one a trumpet player. I can hear my father saying, "Not the lip, don't hit him in the lip!") It would take a saint to be impervious to those influences. My father was not a saint. He took up drinking. Heavily. And before he was 25 he was a problem drinker.

He met my mother in Boston's Normandy Ballroom, and they married a short time later. I was their first child—we traveled as a family with the band for a while. When my mother became pregnant for the second time, she persuaded my father to stop the road work, settle in Boston and look for regular jobs there.

But my father's drinking worsened. I was seven and my brother five when our parents separated, and we were placed in an orphanage. When both parents visited us shortly after Christmas, they found two pathetic boys begging to be taken home. They reconciled and took us out that same day. My father stopped drinking. He was working steadily, and his reputation was growing.

Everything went well until one night in Newport. He was playing for a debutante cotillion and, at a break, got into the champagne punch. When the band reassembled for the next set, the leader called for "The Dark Town Strutters' Ball." My father, as featured first trombonist, stood up for his riff.

He began to play, but it was not the swing arrangement. It was improvisation, spontaneous, jazz. He laid into it, running figure after figure, playing patterns he had never played before, carrying the band with him.

The leader was enraged. "Melody, Bobby, melody," he whispered angrily. And then the alcohol, mixed with anger and frustration, pushed my father's mind over an edge. *Melody?* he thought. I'll give you melody. He concluded his riff, and began playing a chorus in the style of a Sousa march, using his trombone like a weapon, blaring directly at the conductor's head.

Then he stepped back, lost his footing and fell off the platform. He was through for the night, and through with that band forever.

As word went the rounds that Bobby Hohler was unreliable and an ugly drunk, the jobs came less frequently—a wedding here, a smoker there. Often the trombone went into hock to provide the family with a few dollars between gigs.

He took to spending more time in bars than in the union hiring hall. When it grew late, my mother would send me out in search of him. "He's probably down at the corner." The corner was the Back Bay Café, and I would generally find him there. I was nine years old and hungry for the spotlight that he would never fail to shine upon me. He would regale his cronies with stories of my grades in school, the books I read, my memory (he was losing his).

Hours later, he would say, "Well, Bobby, let's go home and face the music." He would stand, unsteadily, place his hat, as always, precisely upon his bald head and let me lead him home.

Then came the Second World War. My father was moving from one defense job to another. The trombone went into hock for the last time. The ticket ran out. There was no more music in our lives.

More and more frequently his condition was one of complete drunkenness. I grew ashamed of him and avoided him as much as I could. By the time I was 14 we were on welfare. We couldn't pay the rent, and one day we were evicted. My mother, brother and I moved into a furnished room, and my father hit the streets to become a panhandler.

At 18, I fled into marriage and began the business of building my own family. But as much as I tried to keep my father out of my life, he still hovered about its edges, a kind of ragged specter, appearing randomly to cause pain, inconvenience, embarrassment. Phone calls at midnight, knocks on the door at dinnertime. He would be standing in the doorway, thin, stooped, a sweat-stained hat placed perfectly upon his head. "I need money. Please." The money would, without fail, go for booze.

I took him to doctors. He wouldn't continue with them. I took him to clinics. He would leave them. I bought him a trombone. He hocked it.

I grew to hate my father. And fear him. Somehow, I felt that he would drag me into the abyss with him.

It is 3 a.m. and I am taking my father to city hospital. He's moaning, "Oh, please, dear God, don't let me wake up in the morning."

I carry him into Emergency, and we sit on a bench and wait. Finally, a resident comes over and looks at him. He shakes his head. "We can't help him here." I explode in anger.

"Listen," the doctor says, "I don't like this any more than you do. But we could fill this hospital up with people like him. We'd be running a grand hotel."

Then his face softens. "I'm sorry. It's been a long night. We have an ambulance going out to Island Hospital in a few hours. We'll put him there." Island Hospital is for homeless invalids, the discards of society. My father had been there before.

He went again—and, during the weeks that followed, a transformation came over him. He acknowledged to himself that he had a deep drinking problem. He joined the AA group at the hospital. His eyes grew clear, and his hands no longer trembled. On my visits we talked future plans. Perhaps he would try the trombone again. Big bands were reviving. "One thing for sure, Bobby. My drinking days are over."

The bitterness and anger I had felt for so many years began to give way to hope. Then, one day, the doctor told me my father had cancer of the liver. In a few short weeks he was bedridden, in deep pain and heavily sedated. His conscious moments were more and more rare.

Tonight, as I sit beside him, he stirs. His body is a tangle of tubes. He is unable to talk, yet I feel he is trying to say something to me. I take his hand and try to read the message in his eyes.

He smiles and draws his hand away. He puts it to his mouth as if he were cupping something; then he begins to move his other hand up and down, up and down. Recognition dawns. He is playing for me, playing the trombone.

All those years of bitterness, grief, hatred and despair are swept away. And I love my father—again.

My Quicksilver Uncle

by Robert P. Tristram Coffin

Uncles are a race apart, created to save children from growing up to be as dull as their parents. They can afford to be natural, where a father can't. Uncles can stuff nieces and nephews with candy and ice cream till their eyes bug out and their buttons pop, for uncles don't have to sit up nights with them. They can teach children to skip school and go to the fair. They don't have to sign the report cards next month.

They are the only creatures in the world, save milch cows and hound dogs, that have leisure. Parents don't have time for their children; they're too busy earning bread and butter or shoes. But uncles have time to sit down and tell stories while fathers sweat. Children don't respect uncles—but they love them.

Uncle Tim, who was my father's youngest brother, was always where life was the thickest, fastest and made the most noise. He was a scapegrace, a teller of tales, the life of every party, a dancer, a fiddler, the pepper and spice and the glory of the family.

My father brought him up after their father died. He tried to tame Uncle Tim to civilization, matrimony and business, but he might as well have tried to slip a halter on the northwest wind, or to hold a drop of quicksilver on a jackknife blade. Quicksilver is alive and changes its plans; it is here, there, everywhere, without warning, and it is gone suddenly into the grass where no one can ever find it again. Uncle Tim was like that.

The stars were against Uncle Tim's holding a job. When my father got him a job in a gristmill, the mill burned to the ground from the cigar Tim always slept with. Father got him a place in the sawmill, but Tim crowded the saw with too big an oak log, and the saw split into a thousand pieces. Tim beat the fragments into the quiet woods and never returned to square accounts with his boss. He was the perpetual small brother, forever getting into hot water and having to be got out of it, but making his older brothers laugh, too.

Uncle Tim could dance anything from an Irish breakdown to a Saracen sword dance. He was double-jointed in his fingers and toes; he could move his shoes faster than sharp eyes could follow. A jig was in his joints and music in his marrow.

He could sing a clear tenor like a wood thrush educated to grand opera, and suddenly shift to a bass like a bullfrog in courting season. He had, too, the gift of whistling two notes at once. He bent in his chin, sparkled and rolled his eyes, did something mysterious with his throat muscles, and out came harmonious high and low notes side by side.

Uncle Tim could play any musical instrument. If there were reeds and tubes, his breath found its way around in them. When he got his mouth on a bass horn, he could make a tame horn player stare at the incredible arpeggios that came out of the brass morning-glory. What he could do with a kitchen cup and a harmonica was something no organ player ever dreamed of. When he clamped his long black mustache, alive as a black-snake, over the honeycomb of a harmonica's edge and played sad, it was like the surf on the last reef of a lost ocean.

He knew songs by the hundreds and made new ones as he went along. Some of his songs were not for she-ears and they made mustached men blush like a field of hawkweed, but Uncle

Tim sang them with the innocent eyes of a boy of ten. He sang also of unrepentant prisoners on their way to the gallows; of girls like anemones, so pure they wilted and died if a man looked their way. His men were all buttocks and beer, his women all tears and true-love knots. And he sang hymn tunes as though they had never seen the inside of a church.

He was the town champion in everything that had legs or fists in it. His long legs could scissor over a five-foot fence with no start. He could throw a man twice his size. He could box an Irish rail-layer to a standstill, then beat an eel of a youth in a hundred-yard dash. He was forever taking off his shoes and shirt to show small boys how to turn seven cartwheels in a row, or do the giant swing.

My Uncle Tim's major calling in life was pranks. He tied a brick to Mr. Snodgrass's cow's tail so that Mr. Snodgrass could milk in peace without getting slapped on the cheek every few minutes, but when the cow swung her tail Mr. Snodgrass fell on the floor and lay in an artificial peace for quite a while.

Tim took the planks off the Widow Nye's dry well, so that when Peter Jordan came to walk out with her, as he had for 20 years, they fell in. They stayed down there all night, and folks talked so, they had to marry the very next day and set up housekeeping above ground.

And it was Uncle Tim who thought up putting bourbon in the raspberry shrub at the Free-Will Baptist picnic. Crowds gathered thicker and thicker at the bowl. The word spread clear to town, and all denominations became Free-Willers for the day. Everybody voted it the best Free-Will Baptist picnic in half a century. It took half the night to collect the Baptists and temporary Baptists and herd them back, singing, to everyday living.

Uncle Tim kept his brothers' and sisters' children bright-eyed and in high animal spirits. He was an artist with a jack-knife, and shocked his sisters and sisters-in-law with the jointed pine-wood dolls he made for his nieces. For he was a realist in his ideas of feminine beauty unclothed. The girls weren't allowed to play with the dolls, which were put away on a high shelf, and the small girls had to grow up into beautiful curves by accident rather than by imitation.

Uncle Tim taught his nephews how to get the best apples from the highest tree with the sternest farmer warding them, how to snake the biggest trout from under the deepest log, how to keep their temper in a fight. He kept people busy straightening out their households after he had paid a call. Their houses would be full of small imitative editions of him, getting their breeches dusted for having soaped the backstairs so that the hired man came down in a hurry.

The first time Uncle Tim ran away was to the Civil War. As far as I can make out from family tradition, it *was* a civil war, until Uncle Tim got in it; then it turned robust, with no holds barred. No general craved having him in his army long. He got into so many side wars along the Potomac that his regiment never could be straightened out long enough to take part in regular battles.

Uncle Tim tried matrimony once. But he was not cut out for a house husband. Maybe if his first-born son had lived, he might have been harnessed to providing the strain of quicksilver men the world so needs. But when the boy he loved died of diphtheria, he gave up family life. He parted with his wife after singing her to sleep with his guitar. He stole out quiet in the night and left the guitar—his best one—for her to remember him by. He did not leave his wallet. There was nothing in it. It was flat as a spring flounder.

One bright October day, Uncle Tim must have felt fall in his bones. Maybe he saw ahead long, quiet evenings beside his brothers' stoves, they expecting him to dance the hornpipe for them and he with no hornpipe left in his legs. He slipped out of their lives when nobody was noting that he had sobered for an instant. He slipped out with a last prank. Father had sent him to Falmouth with a load of mackerel. He sold the mackerel—but he also sold the sloop. With the dollars he never could keep from burning holes in his pockets, he headed into the blue unknown.

A pall fell upon his brothers. They discovered they were aging men. Their houses ached at night with the silence. The ghosts of Uncle Tim's songs hung in the sound the Maine wind made round their houses.

My father, delegated by the brothers to bring Uncle Tim back, put his work aside and followed Uncle Tim's footsteps for nearly a year. Father found a print of his brother's feet once or twice. In a saloon on the Bowery someone from Down East had sung one night like a seraph, making hard men weep. That could be Tim. In a drab Philadelphia waterfront house, a board bill had been paid by stories that made the gray place a shining one. That sounded like Tim. In a lonely Kentucky shack, a family had sat spellbound for three days before such dancing as the nimble mountaineers had never laid eyes on. That might be Tim. The track led south. That would be like Tim: he would have headed toward warmth as he felt his bones growing cool.

But the trail grew colder and colder. My father came back to his business a decade older.

One terrible day, a newspaper described a Maine man who had died in a shabby New Orleans house of smallpox. My father telegraphed and wrote a dozen times. Finally a photograph was secured. It was not Tim. My father grew a decade younger.

A year later there was a man with no name, but a clothier's mark in his coat, who was found dead in a shady Baltimore house. The clothier was from our town—the coat like one Tim had borrowed from my father.

Father went to Baltimore with no light in his eyes. The dead man was a handsome scapegoat but not Tim. Father came home with light back in his eyes.

The years crowded in fast. My father's hair grew whiter, and so did his brothers'. With no Tim to keep them companions they dropped away from one another. So at last most of them dropped into the earth. But the ones remaining remembered Tim's music, dancing and singing. Their sons remembered some of the songs, like *Wait for the Wagon* and *The Old Blue Britches My Grandpappy Wore*. But none could sing Tim's way.

For my father, remembering Tim was like my remembering the jackknife I lost overboard one bleak November day. I saw it slanting down dimmer and dimmer into the dark water where no light ever comes. With it went a bright piece of my heart. It was Tim my father spoke of last, the night he died.

Quicksilver never stays. It runs off your jackknife into the grass. You can look for it among the grassblades till your eyes hurt. It has gone back to the sun where it was born and where it belongs.

*Four Entertaining, Informative Books
From America's Most Trusted Magazine*
READER'S DIGEST

DRAMA IN REAL LIFE
04723-7/$2.50 _____

contains stories of endurance, ingenuity and incredible bravery that take place among real people in unexpected situations.

THE LIVING WORLD OF NATURE
04720-2/$2.50 _____

explores the marvels and mysteries of earth, sea and sky in a collection of distinguished essays by nature specialists.

UNFORGETTABLE CHARACTERS
04722-9/$2.50 _____

is drawn from the highly popular "The Most Unforgettable Character I Ever Met" series, featuring short, amusing tales of both the famous and the obscure.

WORD POWER
04721-0/$2.50 _____

is a fascinating anthology of tests from "It Pays to Enrich Your Word Power," with articles by such language experts as Clifton Fadiman, Edwin Newman and Vance Packard.

Berkley/Reader's Digest Books

Available at your local bookstore or return this form to:
Berkley Book Mailing Service
P.O. Box 690
Rockville Centre. NY 11570

Please send me the above titles. I am enclosing $_____
(Please add 75¢ per copy to cover postage and handling). Send check or money order—no cash or C.O.D.'s. Allow six weeks for delivery.

NAME_____

ADDRESS_____

CITY_____ STATE/ZIP_____ 82

Great Reading on the World's Most Popular Subjects From America's Most Trusted Magazine
READER'S DIGEST

I AM JOE'S BODY   04550-1/$2.50 _____
is based on the most popular series in DIGEST history, in which the various organs of the human body explain themselves

**SECRETS OF
THE PAST**   04551-X/$2.50 _____
explores ancient mysteries and tells about man's earliest adventures.

**THE ART
OF LIVING**   04549-8/$2.50 _____
contains practical and heartwarming advice, designed to help make life richer, more enjoyable, and more meaningful

**TESTS
AND TEASERS**   04552-8/$2.50 _____
is brimful of brain-wracking puzzles, quizzes, games, and tests. It promises hours of escapist fun and mental gymnastics

Berkley/Reader's Digest Books
Available at your local bookstore or return this form to:

**Berkley Book Mailing Service
P.O. Box 690
Rockville Centre. NY 11570**

Please send me the above titles. I am enclosing $_____
(Please add 75¢ per copy to cover postage and handling). Send check or money order—no cash or C.O.D.'s. Allow six weeks for delivery.

NAME_____

ADDRESS_____

CITY_____STATE/ZIP_____